Praise for Feng Chi-shun's previous books

Diamond Hill:
"The harsh but colorful world in which Feng grew up is no more, and the great value of his book is that his story is also, in large part, the story of Hong Kong."
　　　　　　　　　　　　　　　　　　　　　— *Asia Times*

"*Diamond Hill* is an excellent and fast read for those who want an honest depiction of life for a majority of Hong Kong denizens in the 1950s-60s."
　　　　　　　　　　　　　　　　　　— *The Correspondent*

"A highly readable potted history of a part of Hong Kong and its ordinary people in the middle of the 20th century. There is much food for thought on how the challenges of adversity and worldly temptations in childhood make some men, like Dr Feng – and break others, like some of his friends."
　　— John Chan Cho-chak, Chairman of the Hong Kong Jockey Club

Hong Kong Noir:
"If you're interested in Hong Kong's other face – the one that lies on the un-lit side of the city's chrome-and-glass structures, this is probably the book for you. The writer was once part-owner of a dive bar in Kowloon City – where a man who lived on the street could be a secret millionaire and a forgotten movie star could pass himself off as the Elvis of the Orient."
　　　　　　　　　　　　　　　　　　　　　— *China Daily*

"Behind the glitzy, sky-scraping face of success lies an alternate Hong Kong; one of drama and destitution, villains and the vulnerable, chutzpah and chancers. It's the city I knew so well, one Feng Chi-shun writes about masterfully in this long-awaited account."
　　　　　　　　　　　　　— Chris Thrall, author of *Eating Smoke*

KITCHEN TILES

A COLLECTION OF SALTY, WET STORIES FROM THE BAR-ROOMS OF HONG KONG

Feng Chi-shun

BLACKSMITH BOOKS

Kitchen Tiles
ISBN 978-988-13764-9-7

Copyright © 2016 Feng Chi-shun
Edited by Grahame Collins

Published by Blacksmith Books
Unit 26, 19/F, Block B, Wah Lok Industrial Centre,
37-41 Shan Mei Street, Fo Tan, Hong Kong
Tel: (+852) 2877 7899 • *www.blacksmithbooks.com*

Also by Feng Chi-shun
Hong Kong Noir:
Fifteen true tales from the dark side of the city
Diamond Hill:
Memories of growing up in a Hong Kong squatter village

FOREWORD

The Cantonese call anyone lecherous, and anything salacious, *harm sup* – literally, salty (and) wet. And the Cantonese code name for *harm sup* is "kitchen tiles". Anyone who's ever been inside a Chinese kitchen knows it is like a war zone, with water and condiments spilt all over the place; hence the tiles are deemed salty and wet.

Kitchen Tiles is the title of this book because the content focuses on the lascivious aspects of Hong Kong society, and if the articles are not sex-related, they are often off-beat and captious.

Some of the articles were published in the *South China Morning Post* in the late 1990s when I was one of their columnists. Later on, I self-published them with the help of the late Diane Stormont – under the title *Idle Musings*.

Kitchen Tiles is the new and improved edition, with several new stories.

I used the word "bimbo" many times, but all within the same article. I used it not to denigrate women but to show the shallowness of some Hong Kong men. I hope no one gets too upset over its use. I have to forewarn the readers, because when the article appeared in the *Post*, I received some hate mail.

All the stories are based on my life experiences. Names and circumstances might have been fictionalized, but the sentiment and spirit are authentic. There is plenty of irreverence, and maybe some humor. My publisher thinks it's worth republishing my work properly this time. It's up to you readers to prove him right or wrong.

Feng Chi-shun
Hong Kong

CONTENTS

PART I

HONG KONG SPECIALS

I

TEA DANCE

Why settle for just afternoon tea if you can have both tea and dance?

Hong Kong in the '60s and '70s had numerous venues where young people could go in the afternoon for a snack and a drink, and most of all, live music they could dance to. Groups of girls made themselves available as dance partners for young men on the prowl. But they were nice girls, and dancing was all they would agree to. Romance blossomed on a regular basis, I'm sure, but the original motive was solely the love of dancing.

Live bands played Western music, because the popular dances were all Western, including Cha Cha, Rock & Roll, Twist, A-go-go, Two-Step, and Jitterbug. A Waltz sometimes, but rarely Tango.

Then there was another type of tea-dance outlet, which provided in-house dance girls for male customers to choose from, and pay to become their dance partners. Charges were based on the number of units of time spent with the customer, and the duration of each unit varied as widely as the price for the catch of the day. An hour could be divided into twelve, twenty-four, or thirty-six portions, depending on how good the business was at that time. When the service of a lady was hired, she would insert a chit into a container on the customer's table for billing purposes.

In these types of tea-dance places, customers usually went for the slow dance so that they could be physically intimate with the ladies. Groping was not routinely permitted, but because the place was pitch dark, it was frequently attempted. As is usually the case with the flesh trade, the more popular the woman, the less she gave away.

These dance partners were theoretically available for sexual services as well, though many claimed they were doing the dancing part to raise their families, and were not ready to sell their bodies. Many men spent huge sums of money trying to win the hearts of their favorite women so that they could have their bodies as well; but failed, only to find out their friends were able to buy the same women – at a fraction of what they had spent – in a nearby hourly motel where the supposedly chaste women actually worked as freelance hookers.

Interestingly, the steamy environment of such type of tea-dance parlors was the hotbed for the origin of slang commonly used in Hong Kong today. According to legend, in a popular tea-dance outlet in Sheung Wan, a short and ugly patron made up for his deficiencies in the looks department by wearing very expensive suits, made by an up-market tailor on Shanghai Street called Tsuen Tso ("Made by Tsuen"). He was quick to show people the label of his suits when comments were made about his exquisite wardrobe. Soon, he was called *Ah Tsuen,* meaning "an inch" in Chinese, indicating his love of fancy suits made by the famous Tsuen Tso, and also insinuating his small stature and shortness of a specific part of his anatomy as well. *Tsuen* is nowadays synonymous with being cheeky.

Another slang word owing its origin to the tea-dance era is *lo sai,* which is nowadays synonymous with *the boss.* But it was originally used sarcastically to describe another tea-dance patron, who was the boss of a trading company and had a bit of money. He was infamous for being mean, cheap and *harm sup.* He was given to sample every dancing girl available in the dance hall, but was willing to pay as little money for sex as he could get away with. They called him *lo sai* (literally, old and small), because he was ridiculed behind his back as being old in age and small in manhood.

2

LOCKHART ROAD

Lockhart Road in Wanchai never changes.

What remain constant are the sleaze and the sex – a sin city within our metropolis. The atmosphere there somehow attracts many expat male denizens of Hong Kong, and certain tourists.

In the late '60s and early '70s, when I was in my late teens and early twenties, Lockhart Road was a narrow street, made narrower still by the roadside girlie bars pushing their jukeboxes halfway out the door. Over a stretch of many months, they played two songs loudly over and over again – *House of the Rising Sun* by The Animals, and *Black is Black* by The Los Bravos.

Working girls spilled out into the street hustling for business. Typically, the girls wore stilettos, long false eyelashes, dark eyeliners, and lots of make-up – nothing like the girl-next-door image of Nancy Kwan in *The World of Suzie Wong*. Their business hopped when US soldiers took leave from battleships docked in the Hong Kong harbor, in transit to and from Vietnam.

Some of the girls were careless enough to become pregnant, and in Tsan Yuk Maternity Hospital where I was trained as a medical student, the staff at the delivery room often made crude bets on whether the baby coming up would be a black or a white one.

Fast forward to the 21st century.

Lockhart Road is still a narrow street. Old buildings have been replaced by glittering high rises. Neon lights and street lamps are brighter now. The demographics of the women working there have changed radically. It used to be mainly local Chinese; many from the fishing village of Tai O. Now, Filipinas and Thai women are the staple sex workers, with a United Nations of transitory hookers who ply their trade on a short-term basis.

The girlie bars are still there, with young women in hot pants sitting outside the entrance, ogling potential customers and literally pulling them inside the bar if they show the slightest interest. The entrance is usually blocked by a velvety screen, and there is always a metal container nearby, used to hold burning joss sticks and hell money – the traditional practice with any Chinese-owned vice establishment.

These girlie bars are notorious for ripping off the inebriated tourist by adding extra zeros to his credit card bill after he has signed. A tab of $2,500 becomes $250,000 when he receives the monthly invoice back in his home country; too far away to complain effectively to the Hong Kong Police, and maybe too difficult to explain to the wife.

There are also numerous bars meant to be watering holes only. Some ban women who appear to be working girls, while others welcome them by erecting a pole in the middle of the sitting area and providing deejay music to encourage pole dancing – especially on Sunday, the day of rest for many domestic helpers, who want to supplement their income by making trips to an hourly motel close by with any of the drinking customers who are aroused beyond control viewing their pole-dancing moves.

In the wee hours of the morning – notably around daybreak – Lockhart Road could be quite a sight. Among many interesting things, it is not unusual to find an expat man lying next to a pile of garbage by the roadside, in a drunken stupor, vomit all over his expensive tailored suit, wallet empty.

Once in a while, there are police reports of a male customer on Lockhart Road being led to an ATM by a woman, and the man carelessly divulging his PIN to her – apparently after consuming drinks laced with something equivalent to a date-rape drug.

On Lockhart Road, men willingly subscribe to degeneracy, and women excel at hustling money from such men. Just like the good old days.

A friend of mine grew up in the area. He knows a mama-san on Lockhart Road, who started out as a teenage prostitute there. When I was writing another book, he took me to her bar to interview her, for her take on her industry. We spent thousands of dollars that evening buying her and her girls watered-down sugar water. She said she would meet me for lunch the next day to tell me her life story. We even agreed on a rendezvous.

She never showed up.

Lockhart Road never changes.

3

MILLIONAIRES' CLUBS

Special kinds of nightclubs in Hong Kong sell you food and drinks, music and live shows, sex and debauchery, and a chance to blow money like there is no tomorrow. That's why they are nicknamed *siu kum wall*, translated as "money burning pit."

All their customers are men; rich men. You had better be rich if you walk into such a club.

Even the names of these nightclubs suggest exclusivity and decadence: Deluxe, Big Boss, Tycoon and Tai Pan are common prefixes.

Valet parking is part of the game plan to extract money from their clients. For a man to snap his fingers to summon his European sedan, with a beautiful woman clinging to his arm, the tip for the valet is expectantly spectacular, not only to impress the lady but also to ensure there will be no scratches or dents on his expensive car on his next visit.

Inside the club, the decor is glitzy and gaudy beyond imagination. Gold is usually the basic color, and there are more gemstones all over the place than on the costumes of Liberace – the king of bling. Even the toilets are gilded.

The staffers provide courteous service beyond the call of duty; more like fawning and obsequious servitude. The short walk from the entrance to the sitting area is deemed too much hardship for their dear customers; hence, the need for a golf cart remodeled into a mini Rolls Royce look-alike (gold-colored, of course) for the trip.

At one time, the main attraction was infamously the hire of a white man as a lavatory attendant. He agreed to take the job because of promises of incredible tips for handing out paper towels.

The customers pay for all this, and pay they do. The average money spent there a night by a single customer can easily be more than the monthly salary of most local workers. There is no upper limit.

If you are a factory owner with a few visiting buyers in town, and you have to show them a good time as well as show off your generosity and wealth, such a nightclub is the place to go, where you can buy the best and most expensive of everything.

Alcohol is sold by the bottle. Brandy is XO and whisky is also top-shelf stuff. Snacks are exotic and exorbitant – and non-filling.

The ladies for hire are the best in town, in looks and poise. They are required to wear evening gowns, displaying their eye-catching décolletages. If you want their exclusive attention, you can earmark them for the entire evening by paying for their full hours in advance. If you prefer privacy, booths with doors are available at an extra surcharge.

With alcohol, men become boys, and the shenanigans that go on behind closed doors in those booths are legendary. Before the smoking ban, cigars were passed around liberally. When Bill Clinton's tryst with Monica Lewinsky became big news worldwide, games involving cigars and the ladies' private parts were re-enacted by the revelers. The demeaning extra service from the ladies was, of course, appropriately compensated.

Their managers are all expert salespersons, good at coaxing men into spending money to buy "face". And it is made easier after a few drinks. When the XO brandy bottle is half empty, a man tends to loosen his purse strings as well as the belt holding up his trousers.

The mama-sans are important people because they control the girls. If a customer treats them right, by greasing their palms with a five hundred or a thousand dollar bill, he gets the crème de la crème of the girls. The girls make the most money when taken out to spend the night, and that's how most evenings end up for them; earning them at least another few thousand dollars each.

These nightclubs were most popular in the '80s and '90s. The economic downturn in 1998 signaled the beginning of their end. The SARS epidemic in 2003 dealt them a heavy blow, followed by a knockout punch in yet another economic downturn in 2008. Some nightclubs moved to Macau to continue with the tradition. Many downsized to become run-of-the-mill girlie bars.

There are only maybe one or two of them left today, and they are struggling to survive.

The glorious days of these nightclubs live on now only in the collective memories of those who partook in the money-burning saga years ago – be they customers who spent a fortune there, or the workers who made one.

4

BOTTOMS UP

If a club's name has to be telltale and ironic, "Bottoms Up" for a topless joint is a stroke of genius.

The name is subtly naughty – "Bottoms Up" is a word play, but its Chinese counterpart is downright explicit and vulgar – translated into English as "The Naked Buttocks Nightclub".

Opening in the spring of 1971, it was the first topless bar in Hong Kong and by far the most famous, made even more so after Roger Moore used its entrance and neon signs as the backdrop for the 1974 James Bond movie *The Man With The Golden Gun*.

In 1994, a court ruling resulted in its management removing the world-renowned neon signs which displayed composite panels of bare bottoms. In addition, the working girls there were told to at least wear bras and negligees.

It wasn't so prudish in my day, in the early '70s.

I remember that place well.

The club was located in a spacious basement on Hankow Road in Tsim Sha Tsui. Its entrance was narrow but conspicuous because of the neon signs. Inside, the décor was cozy and posh

– more like the inside of a hotel than a home. Carpets ran from the floor to the walls and the sides of the several satellite bars. Mirrors and velvety drapes were everywhere. The lighting was soft and dim.

The satellite bars were hexagonal and small; each tended by a different barmaid. All the barmaids were young and beautiful, and in spite of the club's name, were often topless, but never bottomless. The occasional one wore a bra that was so skimpy it was more like a piece of string hanging loosely across the woman's ample bosom.

The customer – almost always a man – could pick any one of the satellite bars to sit at. His decision was based on availability of a seat, and most of all, on his preference for a particular barmaid. With a drink in hand, and an unobstructed and intimate view of a near-naked beautiful woman who was wont to flirt, it must have been heaven on earth for him.

Most of the barmaids were Westerners, and many were blondes. There was the rare local girl who was less endowed and more modest, and she wore a near see-through bra. The native barmaid's accent was distinctly American – probably from having worked in Wanchai, entertaining American GIs on shore leave. Her "scotch" came out rhyming with "starch".

Even though gentlemen prefer blondes, one had to be careful in that place because not all blonde beauties were what they appeared to be. A few were in fact *yan yiu* – transgender women.

They chose this line of work because, with their surgically or chemically enhanced breasts and heavy make-up, in a dimly lit room, they could easily pass as women, and they didn't have to engage themselves in real sex as required of other flesh trades.

For the uninitiated, it paid to look out for a few things about them before falling head over heels for them. The warning signs were the prominence of an Adam's apple, the size of the wrists, the width of the shoulder, and the histrionics they employed to fake femininity.

To those with discerning eyes, they were quick to confess, and tell their sob stories – such as the need to make quick money for their urgently needed sex-change operations. Such frank admission was amusing, and usually succeeded in deflecting the awkwardness at the moment of the client's enlightenment.

Apart from the more conservative attire, things had not changed much with Bottoms Up since the '70s, and it earned its legendary status over the years – a Hong Kong icon and a must-see institution for many tourists.

Clubs come and go, and Bottoms Up was no exception. It closed its doors in the spring of 2004, succumbing to the escalating rent. By then, it had stayed in business for 33 years!

Its reincarnation in Wanchai was essentially a sports bar. It didn't work; it lasted a mere five years.

5

BROTHEL BRAVADO

The world's oldest civilization might have been the first to glorify the world's oldest profession.

In ancient China, brothels were posh and artistic – good enough for a king. The ladies of the evening were the talented type who could sing, dance, and recite poetry. Warriors stayed there to recuperate from war injuries. Poets, artists, and academics went there to mend their broken hearts and drown their sorrows.

In many Western cultures, men visiting brothels choose to do it alone and in disguise. In Hong Kong, no need. A whole bunch of guys with the same indulgence will organize a party for the event, called "*waiee*" – a slang term loosely translated as "bravado".

Don't know where to go? No worries. Simply pick up a local tabloid newspaper, and there is a whole section devoted to such expeditions.

A few years ago, when Mainland China was trying to curb the flourishing sex trade, the police there would stamp "John" on a Hong Kong man's visa if he got caught consorting with a hooker.

And when he passed through Immigration to get back to Hong Kong, the immigration officers would shout out his "John" status in front of all his fellow travelers. That policy was soon aborted; apparently because the "shame" tactics didn't work at all. The "Johns" often boasted about their experience to their friends.

The kind of men who brag about these types of sex-capades are those who can't tell the difference between buying a woman's body and winning her heart, and are also gullible enough to get all choked up because the girls they procure in a foreign land weep at the airport when seeing them off. I know someone who continues to send money back to his "woman" in Taipei after having had a few brief encounters with her, each of which ended in a tearful farewell at the airport. Because of her superb acting ability, she is getting paid as a concubine without actually having to fulfil the obligations of one.

An ongoing debate among some Hong Kong men is whether it's better to keep a concubine or keep visiting a brothel. Some do both, but many prefer only the latter, which is nicknamed "Instant Noodles". It doesn't require too much imagination to figure out why it is so named, and so much more preferred.

Over the years, gimmicky outfits for the flesh trades have expanded from dance halls to include Wanchai bars, escort services, saunas, karaoke clubs, and "fish-ball" stalls. The fish-ball stalls include massage parlours, wine cubicles, and acupressure centres. First in Taiwan, and more recently in Mainland China, there are barbershops where men go, not for haircuts, but something else.

The dance hall girls' image is that of nice girls doing what has to be done to feed the family. Their first appearance at work used to be called *xia har* or "into the sea", a term now commonly used to describe anyone "venturing into the private sector". To tickle the fancy of the customers, some dance hall owners even described the arrival of a new blood as *virgin xia har*.

The Wanchai bar girls are an extinct breed. Stilettos, heavy eyeliner and long glue-on eyelashes characterized them; *The World of Suzie Wong* glamorized them. They have been replaced by Filipinas and Thai girls wearing hot pants.

Working girls in different kinds of "fish-ball" outlets are collectively known as "fish-ball" girls. They are typically underage karaoke-loving schoolgirls who enter this profession as a summer job at first, but some stay on instead of returning to school.

If you wonder about the name, just go see for yourself how fish balls are made from fish paste.

PART II

BE A SPORT

6

GOLF AND VANITY

Golf balls can float in water? I didn't know that.

But this is a different kind of driving range. Instead of driving the balls into the rolling green, I drive them out into the open sea.

The manager of the driving range in this Manila hotel has reassured me that I don't have to pay for any balls lost. Someone in a motor boat will chase after them and retrieve them. They make special golf balls which float in sea water.

It has been a terrible week at work. The boss (let's call him A.H.) has been at his best again, claiming credit for everything that goes well in the company, and blaming me for everything else.

I needed to get away, before I killed somebody.

My travel agent told me it was peak season, so it would be either Manila or nowhere. I figured that I wouldn't leave the hotel after dark, and I should be safe from bullets from their "Saturday night specials". Now that I've found this driving range, I don't want to leave the hotel at all.

The tee-boy (the manager calls him that) has just brought along two buckets of golf balls with "FLOATING" printed on each one of them. His job is to spot the balls on the tee for me to tee-off, so that I don't have to ever bend down. His name is Ping-Pong (everyone in the Philippines has a nickname). I tell Ping-Pong there is no need to call me "sir". Ping-Pong replies: "Yes, sir." (Everyone calls everyone else sir or ma'am in the Philippines).

Here come two petite and smiling waitresses. (Every woman in the Philippines is petite and smiling.) One is bringing me a towel, the other a cold drink. I take out the Churchill I have brought with me. One lights my cigar, the other runs to get me an ashtray.

I am not a good golfer. Perhaps that is why I have not been able to climb the corporate ladder as fast as that A.H. He says he is a good golfer, but who knows? He also says he is hard-working, competent, and honest. The only quality I can see in him is that he is a good "gofer" for the chairman of the board.

I think I am going to use the 7-iron. I turn around and find Ping-Pong already holding it. I swing. The ball flops into the water a few yards in front of me.

The boat guy zooms by and scoops the ball up with a net, smirking at me for making him go such a long way.

Ping-Pong asks: "The tee too high, sir?" Nope, it's me. The next one is a wide slide. Ping-Pong says: "Good swing, sir." Then the next one is a hook.

Ping-Pong says: "A hook is better than a slice, sir."

I ask Ping-Pong: "Are you good?" He has never hit a ball in his life. The boat guy doesn't allow him. The little twerp, I thought he was an expert.

I am getting better. One almost lands on the boat. The driver ducks just in time. Poor fellow, he should really put on a helmet. Another good one, probably better than anything A.H. can ever hit. He does one thing wrong, an anonymous letter will go to the chairman and he is a goner. I deserve to be the CEO in his place. After all, I am the most talented and hard-working person in the company. With these thoughts, I hit another good one.

All of a sudden, I hear loud applause. I look around and realize that I am the star. The manager is here now with the waitresses and the other tee-boys.

It must be a slow day.

Intoxicated by the cigar and all the attention, I'm now loose as a goose. I hit one good one after another. Here is A.H.'s head, here's his liver, here's his … . Wow, the last one is a rocket. Another round of applause. "You are a tiger, sir," says Ping-Pong. He gazes at me admiringly while putting the last golf ball on the tee. I'd better quit while I'm ahead. That's all for today, thank you. More applause.

I reach for the wad of pesos. I am going to tip big-time. I feel like a CEO. I might as well act like one too.

7

TENNIS THE MENACE

I get to the club early and wait in the parking lot. I hope to waylay Mr. Chang before he gets to the tennis court for our weekly tennis match. I know I don't have to wait long because he is always on time. Right on cue, Mr. Chang arrives in his new Porsche.

I go over and lavish him with compliments about his outfit, even though, name-brand or not, nothing looks good on him. He is a fund manager who has more money than fashion sense. His baggy tennis shorts hang down to his knees, and his tee shirt is one size too small. I have to be nice to him because I want to be his partner today. With a bad hangover, I need all the help I can get.

Mr. Chang is a winner, not because of his backhand or overheads, but his tactics – intimidation and cunning.

When we were first introduced, he claimed with a straight face that he was the father of Michael Chang. But I soon found out that was meant to be a joke. Nobody who plays tennis ping-pong style could possibly be related to Michael. But his style doesn't stop him from winning. He has his ways.

Our opponents are John and Lam. They are good players, but both are meek, and, by nature of their profession (both are dons from a prestigious university), have some integrity. They will be no match against Mr. Chang and yours truly.

Lam needs a lot of warming up. Mr. Chang knows that, so even before we open a can of balls, Mr. Chang tosses a coin and asks: "Heads or tails?" – meaning, let the game begin.

Lam protests that they need to warm up. But Mr. Chang is having none of that because it's already quite late and he has to go to a very important dinner appointment at 7pm. Besides, he says, he hasn't had any warm-up, either.

Before they know what's hit them, we are up 3-0. It's Mr. Chang's turn to serve. He has a generic serve. The ball always gets in, but its speed is probably below the detection range of the radar gun used to measure service velocity in professional tournaments. Still, his serves do a lot of damage because he times them just right – before the receiver is ready. Mr. Chang wins his service game easily. Soon we are up by one set.

The next set is more difficult now that John and Lam are warmed up. We are trailing by 3-1. Mr. Chang held serve, as usual. It is John's turn to serve. He misses his first serve. Now Mr. Chang is at his best. He goes right up to the service line, swings his racket wildly a few times, as if to say, you give me a weak second serve and you're dead. John tries hard to concentrate, but just before he throws the ball, Mr. Chang drops his racket. "Sorry," he says.

John starts over. This time, Mr. Chang does the Three Stooges shuffle, making a lot of noise with his oversized designer tennis shoes. As he always says, it's perfectly legal. Poor John double-faults.

It's 3-3. Then 4-4. Mr. Chang is getting nervous. He comes over and whispers: "They're visibly tired, let's play more dropshots and lobs." But our opponents are tenacious. The rallies become longer and longer, and Mr. Chang and I become tired.

At a crucial point, Mr. Chang hits a ball long by 30 centimetres or so. They call "out". Mr. Chang screams "What?" – as if he has never hit a ball out in his life.

Hands on hips, he marches towards the net. Our opponents are a little intimidated. Lam points to a mark behind the base line. "Where? I don't see it," challenges Mr. Chang. After arguing in vain for a few minutes, Mr. Chang retreats, sulking.

In the next game, I hit one out too, but John and Lam are too intimidated to call another ball out so soon. Lam hits a close one, too close to call, in my opinion, but Mr. Chang calls "out" even before the balls has hit the ground. We argue. But Mr. Chang is magnanimous. "OK, you made a bad call before, we might have made a bad one just now – we're even."

It's 5-4, and we are leading again. John and Lam are so dejected after the last game that they throw away the next one. Game, set, and match. We've won 2-0.

Mr. Chang slaps Lam on the back and says: "You played well today, especially in the second set. 6-3 is pretty close." I remind him it was 6-4. Nope, it was 6-3, he is sure.

It's past 7pm now; what about his important dinner appointment?

"Oh, they can wait," Mr. Chang says with a wave of his hand.

Well, what do you expect from a fund manager?

8

PORTRAIT OF A HORSE LOVER

It has been said that Hong Kong is run by the Jockey Club, the Hongkong Bank and the Chief Executive – in that order.

Horse racing is serious business in Hong Kong. Consider the amount of money involved – up to a billion Hong Kong dollars of punters' money every racing day, two days per week, ten months a year. Most of the profits made by the Jockey Club go back to the community, in all kinds of charity. I ought to know; my contributions have probably covered the cost of two orphanages and three elderly centers.

On any given racing day, half the male citizens of Hong Kong transform into a persona best described as the "Marlboro man". He is cool, moody, taciturn, and he chain-smokes. Don't mess with him. He studies the racing form with such intensity you can feel it from across the street. A favorite position is squatting on the roadside close to the Jockey Club off-track betting center, with the racing form on the ground, freeing his hands to hold a cigarette and explore his nostrils at the same time. Squatting also renders spitting easier and more accurate.

Inside the betting center, the general attitude is: don't explain, don't complain. Pushing and shoving are acceptable behaviour – how else can you get through that crowd? Once in line at one of the windows to place your bets, don't let anyone jump the queue. Not even grandma on crutches. I personally will make an exception if the guy is bigger than I am, and has numerous tattoos on his biceps.

There are other circumstances under which we punters will allow queue jumping. Just the other day, a man ran to one of the windows and asked for the special ticket that accommodated betting in excess of HK$50,000. To the chorus of "oohs" and "aahs", he was offered the opportunity to place his bets immediately. Realizing his hero status, he swaggered to the front. Don't complain, don't explain.

I have my own system for picking the winners. There are many factors to consider. To start with, I use a formula: Winning percentage of horse, times winning percentage of jockey, times winning percentage of trainer, equals the winning score. Naturally, the higher the score, the higher the chance of winning. My formula would have done nicely if the Jockey Club didn't have this habit of interfering – they call it handicapping. They promote winning horses to a higher class, and they make good jockeys carry more weight. I suspect they also try to handicap good trainers too, by making them carry more weight, since most look like they could lose a few pounds.

Always pick the horse whose name you can relate to. I have scientific proof. I have a friend who was born with a smile. We call her Smiley. She bet on a horse called "Smiling" and won a bundle.

There are many other pearls of wisdom in horse-racing: Older horses handle longer distance better, unless they are not in form or injured – and unfortunately old horses tend to be both; positions 3, 4, and 5 win most of the time, but so do the rest; black horses are never dark horses; white horses don't do well on dirt, while brown ones do wonderfully (remember the all-time champion Cigar?); betting by numbers doesn't work; and last but not least, use common sense – in a cup race named after a cognac, you don't think a horse with a French name ridden by a French jockey and trained by a French trainer will do badly.

Punters like to wait for the last minute to place bets – so little time, so much to study; hence the helter-skelter five minutes before every race. I missed a bet once because the guy in front of me – the big guy with the tattoos – was not intelligent enough to fill in the betting tickets correctly, so the girl inside had to help him out with all twenty of them. Death threats were launched by the people behind me. For some unknown reason, some of the threats were directed at me. I sneaked out quickly. I sure didn't want to be around for the results of that race.

As soon as each race starts, there is total silence among the punters, all intently perking up to listen to the race announcer. Then, when the horses cross the finish line, even Marlboro men let their emotions run. Most grunt or swear, and some pump their fists. The classical Marlboro man would go back to the racing form right away. Don't complain, don't explain.

With a system and an attitude, you must wonder how I fare in terms of winnings. Put it this way, I am holding on to my day job.

9

BAR BUT NO DUMB BELL

I have joined a gym. There is nothing wrong with my body, just that my weight needs a bit of redistribution – from my midriff, to my chest and shoulders.

All right, I'll be honest. Another reason I joined is that it is in a hotel, and the membership fee covers three hours of free parking. Now I can lift weights for one hour, and then lift beer bottles for the next two in the hotel bar.

The trainer there is a tough gal. The last time I forgot to put the magazine back into the rack she went berserk and gave me a look that could kill. Who am I to argue with someone whose biceps are thicker than my thighs? The way she pushes us to the limit, with no regard for our lives, reminds me of the movie Ben Hur.

Mr. Liu is here today. He and I have become instant friends, after running side by side on the treadmills a couple of times. In his case, it is more like walking. He suffers from Parkinson's disease and is trying hard to rejuvenate his body after years of neglect.

Mr. Universe – aka Shorty – is here as well. He has this Napoleon complex like you wouldn't believe. It is like saying: "OK, so I'm short, but I'm wide." He virtually lives here, I swear. Mr. Liu and I don't like him. Not that we are jealous of his muscles or anything like that. We wouldn't want to be like him anyway – we prefer having a neck and a paunch.

He is so immature. You know there are no young women around when you don't see Mr. Universe carrying a thick chain which he uses, believe it or not, to tie extra weights to those machines for him to push or lift. Nothing is too heavy for him.

If there are young women around, Mr. Universe will make a spectacle of himself by adding more weights onto his chain and grunting louder and louder, taking a break only to offer unsolicited fitness tips to the ladies, or admire himself in the mirror.

I've been on the treadmill for about half an hour when Mr. Liu starts to wave his arms wildly in the air. That is a signal for me to push the stop button for him. We don't want him to fall again like he did last week.

Poor fellow, I ought to have a talk with the doctor who prescribes this for him. To me, it seems more like torture than a cure, especially with that Amazon slave-driver around.

After regaining his composure, Mr. Liu says: "I wish I was as fit as you are."

"No, no, I am nothing compared to him," I say, nodding towards Shorty. There is nothing like giving your enemy a compliment if you want to fish for derogatory remarks about him.

Mr. Liu obliges. "But you are taller," he says as he rolls his eyes. Big deal; my grandma is taller than he is.

The Amazon is helping Shorty with his routine now. She barks out orders and he grunts in reply. Mr. Liu calls their routine the work-out tango. It's so disgusting to watch I almost throw up.

I head to the far side of the gym, as far away from them as possible. Shorty likes to check on everyone's lifting ability. I don't want him to know that a tall guy like me is only lifting 40 kilograms. It is not getting easier, I can't even do 10 reps. I move the pin to 30kg, but can only do nine. I am so pooped after that I can taste beer.

I must not forget to put the pin to 100kg before I leave in case Shorty comes snooping.

It has not even been an hour yet. Well, I am going to join Mr. Liu in the sauna, then take a long shower. That will take my time in the gym up to about an hour – right on time for the start of happy hour.

10

CEMENT ANALYSIS

What we won't do for a game of mahjong.

CK agrees to be our fourth, but he has an appointment with that public hospital in Shatin to have some tests done at noon; and if we don't mind, we can all meet him in the hospital. When he is finished, we can all go to that mahjong restaurant close by.

I ask CK what he is being tested for. He says it is something called *cement* analysis. (He mispronounces semen.)

They've been trying to start a family for the longest time. CK originally blamed his wife for the infertility, and both he and his mother pressured the wife into taking all sorts of tests to rule out any pathology in her reproductive system. Now that she has been certified normal, CK reluctantly agrees to undergo some tests himself.

When the three of us arrive at the hospital laboratory, the technologist has just handed CK a specimen bottle. I ask: "Where are they going to collect the specimen?" CK rolls his eyes and tells us: "I am going to collect the specimen *myself*, and in *there*", pointing to an "employees only" toilet. "They let me use their toilet because the police might arrest me if I carried out the procedure in the public toilet upstairs," he adds.

James is the only one in our group who has any experience of this kind of "procedure", because he was once a sperm donor. He tells CK that when he did it, it was in a nice room with soft music and plenty of inspirational magazines to choose from. But then, he was donating a service to society and not receiving one, as CK is doing now.

Wong, the callous mahjong aficionado, only worries about when we can start the game. He needs to know how long the procedure will take so that he can call the restaurant to book a table. James says to give him three minutes. CK is offended by the innuendo, because it usually takes him longer, much longer, even in the best of circumstances. We come to an agreement. I will go and get a magazine that will remind him of better circumstances, James will let him use his iPod to listen to soft music, and Wong will call and book a table for thirty minutes later.

When I come back with the magazine, I see CK giving high fives to James and Wong. I suppose he has no need for the magazine after all.

On the way to the mahjong restaurant, I ask CK what his next move will be if the results of his "cement analysis" turn out to be substandard. He says: "That won't happen. I know what I am capable of."

To prove his point, he turns to James: "Hey, remember our trip to Zhuhai last month?" James breaks into a big smile and says: "Yeah, we acted like we had just been released from prison." CK is mixing up virility with fertility.

I tell CK that smoking, drinking, and stress can diminish fertility in men, and ask whether he would consider changing his lifestyle. CK is lost in thought for a little while, then he muses aloud: "Wouldn't it be easier to have a concubine who can bear me children instead?"

PART III

IT'S ONLY A JOB

11

TO LIVE AND LET LIVE

The best way to judge the property market in Hong Kong is to observe the ethos of the real estate agents. Though slick and slimy, by nature or nurture, they are quite easy to read. Simply ask them for a discount on the commission, and see what happens.

In good times, they turn up their noses and move on to the next customer. When things are not going well, they keep talking.

I had to help a non-Cantonese-speaking friend find a place to live around Hollywood Road. He had tried Mid-Levels, but the rent there would eat up most of his salary, leaving just enough money for either food or bus fare, but not both. So Hollywood Road looked better and better every day.

The first thing I asked the agent was how much the commission would be. He said half a month's rent.

I said goodbye.

He said the commission was negotiable, and for me (sir), a special discount of 20 per cent. I opened the door and strategically pushed my friend out. The agent asked: "How about 30 per cent?" I slid my body halfway out the door, when the discount became 50 per cent. I winked at my friend, he nodded, and we walked back in.

The agent found out my friend's budget and lined up a few flats for him to see. For that kind of money, you can only get a 400-500 square foot flat. Most of them have one small living room, a smaller bedroom, a tiny bathroom and a stove. My friend, who is rather tall, frowned at the small bedroom and wondered how his long bed could fit in. The agent had a solution – push the bed through the bedroom door as far as it goes, climb in and out of bed from the living room, and use the rest of the space in the bedroom for a closet.

I translated for my friend, making it clear that was not my idea.

The next flat was on the fifth floor. There was no elevator in that building. The agent suggested a little exercise was good for all of us, and the air would be fresher up there.

The next one was on the second floor. The agent said lower floors were a lot easier to get in and out of. Besides, in case we did not know, moving companies would charge a lot more for higher floors.

The next one was actually an office. It was more spacious than the others. My friend looked around but could not find the bathroom. No problem. The agent took us to the communal toilet down the corridor outside. How could he take a shower, then? The agent recommended using a bucket and a scoop.

In every flat, the agent would volunteer innovative ideas as to how the furniture could be arranged. "You put the sofa here, the TV stand in the corner, coffee table here, a refrigerator across, a sound system against that wall, a dining room set here, a mini bar there ..."

He was using each wall and corner three or four times.

I stopped translating for my friend after a while, because I saw blood in his eyes.

My friend took the first flat. Putting half the bed in the bedroom and the other half in the living room was not such a bad idea after all.

No matter how much we despised our agent, we had to admit he had served our purpose well. It is a loathsome way to make a living, but someone has to do it.

I2

GABBY CABBIE

No matter how you look at it, taxi drivers represent a cross-section of Hong Kong's working class. Although they share ethos and pathos, they are not all the same. Once in a while, you come across a "character".

I ran into a gabby cabbie the other day. He had his flag covered by the OUT-OF-SERVICE sign. But he came over after I made a signal with my hand which indicated going under the sea and up again – the universal cross-harbor sign which my wife calls the Submarina Dance.

After confirming that I was going cross-harbor to Kowloon, he released the locked door to let me into his cab.

He took one look at me and said: "You look very educated, not like me. I didn't even finish primary school. I only know a handful of words. My English is especially bad, I only know *yessy* and *lo*."

His attitude implied: "I'm illiterate, and proud of it".

How did he obtain his taxi-driver's license, then? "My cousin took the test but put my name on the application form. Well, that was many years ago."

Then he went on to tell me his life story, whether I wanted to hear it or not. The poor fellow was physically abused by his father, treated badly by the relatives he had to stay with because his father did not want him around, and was frequently punished by his teachers for poor grades. He escaped by going to work as an apprentice in a leather factory, becoming his own man at the age of 13. He decided to pursue a career in transportation, and obtained his driver's license when he was 18. And the rest was history. There was smugness in his tone, which could be translated as: "Yeah, but look at me now."

I could not help but be uncouth and ask the most commonly asked question in China: "How much do you make?" He was earning close to HK$50,000 a month. Yes, I heard it right. He had owned the taxi license for about 10 years. He worked one shift, and leased the other to his cousin – the same one who helped him with the written part of the driving test.

"With all that education, are you making loads of money?" he reciprocated.

I told him that I was a writer and it would be too embarrassing to tell people how much I was paid.

Why the hurry to go back to Kowloon? It was dinner-time at home with his wife in Whampoa Gardens. "You live *there*?" I asked a rhetorical question and found myself sounding stupid.

He owned their home in Whampoa Gardens. Now that the children had gone to university in Canada, they actually had two spare rooms in the flat.

The two children were studying computer science and business. He did not want them to drive a taxi for a living like he did. No prospects, he said.

When we had almost reached my destination, he asked whether he could drop me off at the main gate instead of driving all the way to my building through a narrow lane and the parking lot. The reason? He was only good at going forward, but not at backing up.

YOUR MONEY OR YOUR LIFE

An insurance broker has to be a good actor and manipulator to be successful. The world then becomes his oyster.

I bought some life insurance from a friend of a friend's relative about a year ago. Not that I needed it, but I was held to ransom by the slick operator.

I told him I did not need any life insurance now that my children were old enough to look after themselves, and that I had a few bucks tucked away for my funeral when the inevitable happened. He said: "You still need some protection; I worry about you."

After hours of fruitless persuasion, he changed tactics. First he sighed, then he let me in on a secret. He was a contender for an award for the salesman of the year, and he needed to sell one more policy to make it. Without that award, his future would be bleak. His voice started to crack and his eyes became watery. I was moved to tears. I was looking at a fine young man trying to win an award, and establish himself as a useful member of society. If I deprived him of that opportunity, he might lose his job, and start robbing people in the street.

I had no choice but let him rob me of a year's premium. That was a year ago.

Last week, I got a call from him, reminding me that it was time to renew my policy. I told him no, because I never really needed it, and I had bought a policy from him last year only to help him win an award. He said: "But you need some protection." He called again the following morning and said: "We must talk." That was why I ended up in a restaurant, waiting for him.

Here he comes, walking and talking on his mobile phone at the same time. He gives me a firm handshake and a broad smile. I waste no time and tell him once again that I do not need any life insurance. The only assurance I need after I die is a proper burial, for which I have saved some money, although that fund has dwindled considerably since last year because of the insurance payment.

He is beginning to look that way again – lips trembling, voice cracking, and eyes teary. He has another secret to share with me. The way the award works is that he has to keep his clients for at least 13 months, otherwise he will lose a lot of points (money?).

Here we go again. I try hard to think of a compromise, but he has come well prepared. Apparently he has already consulted his supervisor, and they have worked out a more affordable policy for me. Then he takes out a chart and a pocket calculator, and does some serious calculation.

He is offering me a cheaper policy, but he warns me: "The cover is less." He adds: "I've been working hard to come up with this unique policy so that you are protected."

I reply sarcastically: "I owe you one then." He may or may not have heard the remark because his mobile starts to ring. He says he will be on his way to meet another client in a few minutes, so he has time only for the other half of my sandwich.

Guess who picks up the tab for the meal.

14

ON GUARD FOR A CUSHY JOB

The old man who guards our building is finally retiring.

I heard it from the horse's mouth yesterday when I left home for work. I was pleasantly surprised when he greeted me with a "good morning" – and it wasn't even close to Lunar New Year yet. Throughout the years he would only become friendly in the week before New Year, no doubt for the *lai see*. He told me the new legislation had forced him to retire because of his age, and next month would be his last.

I have mixed feelings about his departure. On one hand, I will probably miss the face of a grumpy old man perched behind the booth facing the entrance to the building; on the other hand, he is not very good at his job. He cannot possibly be good, because he sleeps through most of it.

Sometimes I feel like playing a trick on him by lighting up a firecracker and throwing it his way; but instead, my wife makes me tiptoe while passing his booth for fear of waking him up.

Besides, he has been abusing his position by using that booth as his apartment, where he stores all his worldly possessions. He also cooks all three meals, and of course, sleeps there. The public toilet not far from our building serves him more than anyone else in the neighborhood. Among other things, he does his laundry there.

On his days off, he becomes more energetic. He is a regular among the chess players in the park next to the public toilet. You should have seen him arguing with his opponent and all the onlookers when he reneged on a move he had just made.

His only function is being an information exchange center for the tenants.

When you pass by – provided he is not napping – he makes unsolicited announcements of what goes on in your neighbors' lives. Last week alone, I learned that Mrs. Chang in 3A was leaving for Canada; 5D's daughter would be getting married next month; and Mr. Lee in 4C had just bought a new washing machine.

I might have liked him more if it were not for the time he railroaded me when I sought his help in getting rid of some old furniture. He made a project out of it. He came over to our flat to inspect the furniture, checked the brand, and took measurements. Then he charged me a removal fee. This was fine. But then I found out later that he had actually sold the furniture to the young guy who did the moving for him.

My wife thought he was a true Hong Kong entrepreneur; I thought he was a scoundrel.

I asked him what his plans were after retirement. Apparently, he has saved enough to have built a house back in his hometown in Guangdong, and he intends to move there soon. He also wants to continue to work.

I hate to tell him so, but I don't think he can find a job over there as cushy as this one.

15

HARD KNOCKS CAFÉ

Yesterday, I had a meal in a *Cha Chaan Teng*, the unique type of Hong Kong restaurant which over the years has been gradually replacing another iconoclastic Hong Kong eatery – the al fresco *dai pai dong*.

Many of my expatriate friends complain about the service in *Cha Chaan Teng*. They think it is a racial thing. Nope. Trust me, they treat everyone equally badly.

My waiter was not a proponent of the "Keep Hong Kong Clean" slogan. You could tell he had not had a shower in the morning, because the hair at the back of his head was flat in the center, spiking out around. He also had hair in all the wrong places, such as sticking out from his nostrils, and a big mole on his cheek. Like many others of his genre, he had cigarette-stained teeth and tattooed arms.

He put a glass of water in front of me on the filthy table. When I asked him to please clean the table first, he grabbed a gray towel and made cursory motions around the glass, missing a large grease spot and a piece of noodle hanging from the edge of the table.

All the while, he had his head turned to one of his colleagues and was gabbling non-stop about horse racing. It was impossible for me to get a word in.

"I'll have the set lunch, option C," I said. The place was noisy, and he did not indicate whether he had heard me or not, as he scratched his mole and kept talking to someone else. So I repeated myself.

Apparently I had somehow offended him by repeating my order. He replied sarcastically: "Do you want two orders of that?"

As he brought my meal, I fixed my eyes on him all the way from the kitchen area, to make sure his thumb did not dip into my soup. I have heard horror stories about what waiters do to their customers' food for revenge.

The food was OK, even though I would have preferred my entree served before my dessert and coffee.

I was quite grateful that the waiter had left me alone, and the food, as far as I could see, had not been tampered with.

I was also grateful the two families that the waiter arranged to share my table when I was having my soup had found their own tables by the time I was almost finishing my dessert.

It was time for the tab. From past experience, I knew I would have about 1.5 seconds to grab my change before it became a tip. They don't leave the cashier's tray on the table. The waiter holds it slightly above your eye level, always ready to pull it away. I thought I had better plan a strategy first.

The set lunch was $68. If I gave a $100 note, I should get back $32. Would it be a ten and a twenty and change? Unlikely. It would probably be some five-dollar coins and many twos and ones. So I would have exactly 1.5 seconds to grab back at least two or three five-dollar coins first and hopefully some of the twos and ones.

What if it was all one-dollar and two-dollar coins?

By the time I had worked out all the possible combinations of $32 in small change, I was a nervous wreck.

I was able to get back $18. I missed catching the rest of the coins by a fraction of a second as my anxiety got the better of me.

My waiter became friendly right after I had paid the bill and he asked whether the English racing form I was reading was any good.

Now that I had finished my meal, I had no fear. I could play a trick on him.

I told him it was a "can't lose" racing form and that I had already made $50,000 since the beginning of the season.

I placed the form on the grease spot on the table and pointed to one of the worst tipsters in history.

"Follow him," I said, "I'm finished with the form, and you can have it."

"That'll teach him," I thought.

PART IV

Bum Deals

16

IN PURSUIT OF HIRSUTISM

My wife hears my scream and rushes to the bathroom. Seeing me all shook up and pale as a ghost, she sits me down and pours me a shot of brandy.

I point to the heretofore non-existing bald spot at the crown of my head, and scream: "Tell me this is not real, tell me this is not happening." My wife tells me it's real and it's been happening for at least a few months, just that she has not bothered to share that information with me. She says: "No big deal, people don't even notice it unless you bend down, or you sit while they stand."

Thanks for the warning – I must remember not to do either of those things in public.

I break out into a cold sweat when the nurse tells me on the phone that it will be two weeks before I can have an appointment with the specialist doctor. It's my life's major crisis and they don't care enough to see me right away.

My wife is unsympathetic. She says it is not an emergency, not any more so than her headache last week, for which I procrastinated taking her to the neurologist because of a marathon mahjong contest.

She says: "Just like what you said about my headache, maybe that hair problem of yours is all in your head."

She is such a clown, but I am not in the mood for laughs. I have to make a list of all my hair-challenged friends, and call them one by one for advice. My wife says: "There is no point. If they could help, they wouldn't be on your list."

So I start to make a list of friends with lots of hair. My wife offers unsolicited advice: "Don't call them. You know what they are going to say – Hi! I'm Harry, and you're not." She is right. I'm not in the mood for that either.

My neighbor Bert is balding. He may be the perfect person to guide me through this personal catastrophe.

Bert sighs and says philosophically: "You just have to work with what you've got. Keep the hair on your sides long and hide your bald spots by creative combing. Also, your hair covers more ground if it's wavy and curly."

I can just see myself fighting with my wife over rollers and the curling iron.

I am looking for a magic cure, so I ask Bert: "How about that lotion they advertise in the newspaper?" Bert says: "I have tried them all. Trust me, don't waste your money." He advises me to seek hair-weaving treatment if I am desperate enough. But that is not without risk, and the hair looks almost natural only on a clear windless night.

There is also hair transplant technology, if I don't mind spending mucho money. He says men go for transplants only when the balding process is end-stage, otherwise it is like trying to fill a bottomless pit. I tell him to stop using the word end-stage when he talks about my condition.

I don't feel any better after that conversation, so I call up my father, who doesn't look bad for someone his age, and ask him for advice. He says: "Don't worry, son. Your bald spot will become less conspicuous when what's left of your hair turns white."

I ask him about the popular word-of-mouth treatment by rubbing brandy on the bald spot. He says: "You might as well drink the brandy."

Just what I need. Thanks, dad.

17

LAI SEE

I am always a nervous wreck a week or so before Chinese New Year (CNY). I always have to pull my hair out trying to find the balance between doing the right thing and going bankrupt from giving out *lai see* during the first two weeks of CNY.

The security guard, who usually denies my existence, starts to treat me like a human being around then. I wish I had been brave enough to snub him by not giving him any *lai see* last year, and be prepared to put up with his snooty attitude for the rest of the year.

If I could have it my way, I would celebrate my New Year by throwing a string of firecrackers his way when I caught him napping in his booth.

My next-door neighbors also put pressure on me around this time of the year. The matriarch of the Lau family – I call them the "loud" family – makes her bratty children call me *uncle* whenever we meet by chance in the hallway or in front of the elevator. Heaven forbid – I do not want to be related to them so please don't "uncle" me. One year, I gave her children a $10 coin each.

As soon as they felt a coin in the red envelope, they rolled their eyes, and probably made faces at me behind my back.

Replacing the $10 bill by the coin was one major government foul-up. That policy caused inflation to rise by 100 per cent in many households that year around CNY. Thank God we again have the ten dollar paper money again, just to get those snooty kids off my back.

I also have to take care of the people in the *Cha Chaan Teng* where I go for meals just about every week.

There must be more than 20 people working there. With their dirty smocks and messy hair, I find it hard to tell them apart. I hope I won't make the mistake of giving some of them *lai see* twice and some none at all. If only one of them holds a grudge, I will not be able to walk into the place without worrying about my food being sabotaged.

It is just as hairy in the office. According to tradition, if you are married, you are obligated to give *lai see* to those who are younger and single. Some of my co-workers might have remained single all these years just for that reason.

I could emulate George, who can hardly speak English but still claims to be too Westernized to follow any Chinese tradition.

Or I could do what CT had confessed to last year – giving out empty red packets. With all the commotion going on when everyone is either giving or receiving a whole bunch of them at the same time, who would know where each red packet comes from? Meanwhile, I can divert any suspicion by spreading rumors about CT doing it again.

Another option is to skip town for a while, until the festivity dies down. That means having to disappear for two weeks or more – quite difficult for a salary man like yours truly.

There is no way out.

It's karma. It's pay-back time – for all the *lai see* I badgered out of grown-ups when I was a kid.

18

A SUNNY DISPOSITION

A Chinese saying goes like this: "A fair complexion hides ugliness three times over." For thousands of years, this conventional wisdom has led millions of Chinese women to avoid the sun at all costs.

Not too many years ago, when walking was a principal mode of transportation in Hong Kong, it was common to see women carrying umbrellas to block the sun while walking.

I heard it was the same in old Europe – the fairer the better. Having a tanned skin in those days labeled you as the peasant type who had to toil in the fields under the sun.

When I was a kid, my father told me the way to tell Englishmen and Americans apart was that Americans were always tanned. I assume it was the Americans who first thumbed their noses at the orthodoxy by deliberately baking their light skin brown. Then came the Beach Boys, who extolled the virtues of sand, surf, and sun. Their songs mesmerized first the Californians, then the rest of the world, and people started soaking up the sun like it would never come out again.

Nude beaches are there because I guess there are people who, among other reasons, prefer to be tanned all over. I've always wondered if nude sunbathers assume awkward contortions of their bodies so that even "where the sun don't shine" can receive the same amount of sunshine. If they do, I don't want to be there.

In Canada, where summers are short, and sunny days are few and far between, my wife's relatives would take a day off and do nothing but sunbathe whenever the weather is sunny and warm. Rumour has it some of them even slap butter on before baking their bodies under the scorching sun.

According to my Aussie friends, teaching is a popular profession in their country because teachers get the whole summer off. Not a bad deal indeed – stay snug and warm in the classroom when the weather is miserable, and transform into a beach bum when the sun is bright and the sky is blue.

Too bad there are too many sun-related health hazards.

It is ironic that you are supposed to look healthy when tanned, but in fact, you are anything but. The sun single-handedly causes skin cancer, wrinkles, freckles, so-called liver spots, and many other aging skin problems. Chronic sun exposure makes you look older than your age. The fountain of youth is definitely not found under the sun.

Being tanned is like being rich. While the rich get richer, tanned people get more tanned easily. I am born with a tan, and I can get more tanned without even trying. At my age, I don't care that much about hiding my ugliness behind a pale skin, but

I am health-conscious. I don't need another cancer risk. That's why I avoid the sun like the plague. My wife on the other hand embraces it.

Last weekend we went to the beach. The weather wasn't perfect because the sun was playing peek-a-boo with the clouds. I hid under the umbrella. As usual, my wife found a spot where the sun was totally unobstructed.

At the end of the afternoon, my wife was still as pale as a *gwai poh*, and I got a serious tan from reflected sunlight from the sand.

Neither one of us was happy.

19

STOGIE STOOGE

"That thing smells like what it looks like, and you put it in your mouth?" This is the kind of remark I have to put up with all the time. That is because I belong to a club whose members are all social outcasts. People ostracise us, harass us and ban us from their homes. And our only wayward behavior is – smoking a cigar.

I remember exactly how I started this disgusting habit. I was in a hospital visiting a friend whose wife had just had a baby. He told me that after what he had been through in the waiting room the night before, he felt like taking a break from the hospital and having a cigar.

I asked: "What about your wife?"

He said: "Oh, she doesn't like cigars."

That settled it. He and I went to a pub nearby to smoke, and drink brandy.

It was great fun. I still remember the camaraderie, and the fact that he actually asked *me* for advice regarding child rearing, spousal relationships, and life philosophy in general. The stinky smell of cigars bonded us that night and we have remained cigar buddies ever since.

Over the years I gathered more and more buddies who shared the same passion. It is easy to become friends if you are the only two among 100 people to smoke one of those at a social function, especially when the other 98 are making you feel uncomfortable by giving you dirty looks, or pinching their noses and coughing violently.

Cigar smokers gravitate towards one another for the sole reason of seeking solace, and perhaps protection (safety in numbers?) from the rest of the world.

As my cigar knowledge grows, I become more and more snobbish towards "amateurs". When I started, I was taught by a red-neck to dip the mouth end of the cigar into red wine or brandy before lighting up. That is a no-no. And there is no point in holding the cigar to your ear while kneading it with your fingers. Both practices do nothing but ruin a fine cigar.

Another uncouth habit of the uninformed is to lick the wrapper of the cigar from top to bottom before lighting up (supposedly to glue it down). A friend of mine looks comical whenever he does that. While he is covering his cigar with spit, his upper eyelids go up and down in synch with the movements of his big fat tongue – reminiscent of a cat cleaning some far-reaching parts of its anatomy.

Another thing that we aficionados do to annoy others is that we do not stub out the cigar when we are finished. Only we know that it takes just as long to extinguish if left alone, and it smells worse if stubbed.

The label on the cigar used to be there to prevent men from getting their white gloves dirty. It is now a status symbol. I tear it away if it gives away its origin anywhere other than Cuba. If it says Cohiba, I flash it all over the place.

But I will say one thing, though – in the words of a famous politician, I have never inhaled. Most cigar smokers don't.

That begs the question: If the cigar smoker annoys so many people, pays big bucks for their cigars, suffers from halitosis and oral-cancer risk, and he doesn't even inhale the smoke to enjoy it, why does he keep doing it?

20

A CURE FOR THE SUCKER BUG

"Lady, can you do me a small favor? Watch these boxes for me for a little while, and I'll reward you with two hundred dollars.

Oh, you want to see what's in there first? Fair enough. Let me show you. These white tablets are medicines recently invented by scientists from the Chinese National Science Institute and are a sure cure for the SUCKER bug. You've heard of it, haven't you? I don't know what has become of this world. First the AIDS virus, then the Chicken Flu and SARS, and now . . . the SUCKER bug.

I am fortunate enough to have got hold of some of these wonder pills because I have a cousin who is a top cadre from Beijing. Only people like him can get hold of a national treasure like this. You know what I mean? I am on my way to meet somebody who is going to pay me $200 for each tablet, and I have 5,000 tablets in here.

I need to go to the toilet. It's filthy in there and I don't want to bring these boxes with me. I won't take long. Here is $100, another $100 when I come back out. I'm a good judge of character, and I know I can trust you. Be right back."

*****

"Lady, aren't these the pills for the SUCKER bug? I recognized the label right away. Holy cow! I've been looking for them for weeks. You know how hard it is to get hold of them, now that the SUCKER bug will strike anytime soon.

Can you sell me some? I'll pay you good money for them. Tell you what, I will pay you $400 for each pill, and I want 2,000 of them. Yes, I'll pay in cash. My bank is in Mong Kok, and I'll be back with the money in less than half an hour. You must promise me that you'll sell me 2,000 tablets. Anything less, no deal."

*****

"Lady, here's your other $100. I have to leave now, thanks for watching my stuff.

You want to know whether I can sell you some of these wonder pills? Oh, you have a cousin who has just come down with the SUCKER bug. That's too bad, because I am on my way to see a buyer now.

Well, you sound desperate, and I'd like to help you since you are such an honest person. I mean, you could have taken the whole lot while I was in the toilet. Let me try to talk my buyer into taking only some now, and the rest on my next shipment.

Meanwhile, show me the money. Yes, 2,000 at a bargain price of $200 each would cost you only $400,000. I'll call my buyer while you go get the money from your bank. Hurry back, before he changes his mind."

*****

"No, I don't need to count the money. I knew you were someone I could trust the moment I laid eyes on you. Here they are ... your 2,000 tablets. I must go now, while you wait here for your cousin to come."

*****

The lady waits, and waits, and waits . . .

PART V

OUT OF HONG KONG

21

BITING THE BULLET

What can you get for the man who has everything, in a backwater place like Saipan, that you cannot get in Japan? The answer: A gun with real bullets.

That is the niche market someone has discovered. Billboards everywhere advertize in Japanese: "REAL BULLET SHOOTING."

I saw one across from my hotel room and stayed up all night debating; should I or shouldn't I? Finally, common sense prevailed. Like learning to swear and losing one's virginity, handling firearms is a manhood thing we men must be initiated into – the sooner the better.

The ad directed me to a department store on the ground floor of a shopping center. The moment I mentioned guns, two shopkeepers rushed towards me; one with a menu, the other with a cash register strapped to her back. The menu read: Plan A - four rounds with a semi-automatic rifle; Plan B - four rounds with a Magnum; Plan C - four rounds with a shotgun; and Plan D - a combination of the above.

I told the menu girl that I had never touched a gun before, and asked what I should choose. Thumping her chest with her fist, she replied: "The shotgun of course. Boom boom boom. Real man."

But a street-smart guy like myself would not be so easily taken for a ride. Never take what a vendor recommends. So I took Plan D – the smorgasbord – thank you.

It cost US$65.

It turned out the shooting range was nowhere near the department store. A handsome Filipino man came in and pointed to an old pick-up truck outside.

"Only five minutes away," he said.

I was a little wary of the sleazy way the business was conducted, as I followed the driver-cum-shooting-instructor outside. Then I saw two meek-looking Japanese gentlemen already sitting at the back of the truck. Hey, a man's got to do what a man's got to do. I stuck out my chest and swaggered towards them.

The shooting gallery was nothing like what I had anticipated. It was dark, small, and rustic. No cocktail waitresses. The driver-cum-instructor was the janitor as well. He tidied up the place, laid three firearms and some cartridges on the bench top in front of each one of us and started the lesson.

"This is the semi-automated rifle; this, the Magnum; and this, the shotgun."

"Boom boom boom," I said, quick to show off my knowledge of firearms in front of the Japanese contingent.

The instructor then said: "Aim and shoot." End of lesson.

For people like me, without physique, stamina, or mental fortitude, firing a gun was always a cinch. I knew, because even before I started shooting, the instructor told me I was a natural, just from the way I was holding my firearms. He lavished so much praise on me it was embarrassing.

First I did the semi-automatic, then the Magnum, and finally, yes, the boom boom boom. The whole thing was over in three minutes. Our targets were close, and all my shots were on target. They could have moved my target a lot further away. Obviously, my ability was grossly underestimated.

Interestingly, each of our targets was a sheet of cardboard with a sketch of a woman printed on it.

"Men shoot better at women," our instructor confided in us. We all nodded knowingly.

The cardboard target was given to us – a certificate of proficiency of sort.

On the way back, I asked my Japanese comrades whether it was their first time. One of them held up five fingers. No wonder they were carelessly folding and crunching their certificates; they each had four other ones like that back home.

After slapping each other's back, I bid farewell to my macho buddies.

I was US$65 poorer, but then, a man's got to do what a man's got to do.

22

HOMECOMING CHUMP

Everyone likes to visit his or her hometown, and I am no exception.

Again and again, I would pay big bucks for a trip down memory lane – which might not even be that pleasant. Still smarting from my last visit when someone stole my camera, I went back again last week.

The plane ride was something else. I was nonchalant about the chaos and lack of safety discipline on China Airlines, and I didn't mind every passenger except me having four carry-ons; or even that awful guava-juice and mixed-nuts dinner. But when I saw smoke coming out from the back of the plane, I became quite emotional.

I was saying my third "Hail Mary" when the stewardess explained to another concerned passenger that the smoke was from one of the crew members cooking a bowl of noodles for herself.

After I checked into the four-star hotel – which would be one-star by any other standard – I went out for a walk.

A shoeshine woman followed me for blocks. I firmly declined the service because I was wearing my "China shoes" – weather-beaten and suited to the dusty roads of China. Then she ambushed me and smeared some white wax on my black shoes. So I changed my mind and agreed to it. What was I supposed to do, walk around all day like that?

It would cost me five yuan (HK$6). That was fine. Then another woman came from nowhere and started on the left shoe while the first woman was working on the right. So the charge was actually five yuan per shoe.

She did say what I wanted to hear after I handed over the money. She said her children were starving and that I had the heart of Buddha.

After that ordeal, I was ready for a beer and that famous spicy beef dish. I found myself in an *al fresco* "home cooking" restaurant. (They all are). The beer was good and the beef even better. I was having a wonderful time sitting by the roadside at a busy intersection watching the world go by.

The only distraction was that every few minutes a stranger would come by without making any eye contact, and whisper with a hand over his mouth: "I have an unbelievable deal on antique [or jade, or herbal medicine, or whatever]." Then he would retreat quickly into a corner close by with his back turned, puffing on his cigarette and waiting for my response. At one point, there were six or seven of them around my table, all with their backs turned, and all ready to spring into action if and when I showed any sign of interest.

Then a three-wheeled passenger bicycle came by, manned by a beer-drinking cyclist who stopped his bike by the curb and yelled: "I can take you sight-seeing, and you pay me whatever you think is fair."

I was quite pleased with his arrival, since he eased the tension created by the numerous predators around me. Besides, I could have used a beer buddy at that time. He commented on my mastery of the local dialect, and wondered if I was in town visiting relatives. I told him all my relatives had skipped town in the 1950s. He thumped his chest with his fist and said: "I'll be your relative."

He came over to my table, sat down and ordered himself a beer on my tab. Now that my "cousin" had arrived, all the predators disappeared.

After a few beers, on top of what he had consumed earlier, my "cousin" was bad-mouthing all the Chinese leaders, past and present. His biggest gripe was that the best years of his life were wasted in ideology when he could have been building a better life for himself and his family.

He insisted on giving me a ride back to the hotel. I told him it was unnecessary because the hotel was just around the corner. I did not tell him that, but I was afraid to be the first known victim of a drunk-riding accident. He left me his email address and asked for mine, promising to write; and I left him 100 yuan. What were cousins for?

I read somewhere the reason the collapse of the "bamboo curtain" did not result in an economic catastrophe for China was the continued financial support from overseas Chinese.

I did what I could.

23

LUCKY YUAN

Our government didn't know what to do with all the land in Qianhai, between Shenzhen and Hong Kong's New Territories, which was earmarked for commercial developments. So it followed the time-honored formula – if in doubt, build a theme park.

I have seen it coming ever since that theme park in Qianhai had a grand opening a month ago. My in-laws from Wuhan are here to visit and all four of them cram into the small guestroom.

I am not bitter or anything like that, but they never bothered to visit on our 20th wedding anniversary last year, or when I had my gallbladder removed the year before that. Now they are saying that they have really missed us. I bet. If they had missed us that much, why were they all holding three-day passes to the theme park when they showed up at our door?

I am not proud of my in-laws. They are all theme park addicts. They've been to all the theme parks in the world, including the five Disneys and Hong Kong's Ocean Park. The patriarch is about my age, but still wears shirts and ties with prints of Disney cartoon characters. It you ask me, he looks ridiculous wearing that hat with two black flaps behind the ears. And the matriarch calls both her children by their Disney nicknames – Mickey this, and Minnie that.

I desperately looked for an excuse not to go to the theme park with them. I was faking abdominal pain and was willing to go as far as having an appendix operation. But my wife gave me a look that almost did me in, and ordered me to get ready.

Our new Chief Secretary came up with the name Lucky Yuan in Qianhai, a word play on *yuan's* double meaning, a park or the renminbi – a Yuan with Chinese characteristics indeed.

This Yuan is different from all the rest. For one thing, they have games to cater for Chinese people from around the world, such as the "Hong Kong Monopoly," which is based on the ups and downs of the Hang Seng Index and the Hong Kong property market during the past 30 years. I send my brother-in-law over to play the game, tipping him: "Sell everything right after the handover in 1997, and again before SARS in 2003."

My wife and her sister go for the Chinese opera make-up contest. After that, they will go to "Virtual Diva" – a hi-tech karaoke game where you can perfect your singing by working on a computer.

The kids go for the rides. I recommend the one called "The Stanley Bus Ride". The kids whine: "But we want something scary." I say: "Trust me."

Another feature of this Yuan is that there is no need for queuing at any of the rides. Queue jumping is allowed, and fighting to get a place on any of the rides is part of the fun.

I pick up the candle wrappers and paper cups the kids have thrown on the ground and go to the "garbage-throwing" game. This game is the brainchild of a Hong Kong legislator nicknamed "Dr. Garbage." You go to a fenced-off area with many refuse bins inside and you lean over and throw your garbage into the bins. If you don't spill any of the trash on the floor, you win a can of milk powder. Many people still miss and leave garbage outside the bins, but at least the rest of the Yuan is clean.

The workers in Lucky Yuan are polite and nice. They are all graduates of the Disney School of Hospitality. Some are going overboard with friendliness. The girl behind the fast-food counter greets me with: "Hi! My name is Debbie. What is yours?" I ignore her.

I see my brother-in-law approaching, flushed with excitement. He screams: "I've won four season tickets to Lucky Yuan".

I scream.

24

WEEKEND RETREAT

I love visiting Macau, I've always had fun there.

Except for that one time.

It was a few years before its handover, when Macau had become a battleground for triad societies.

With the murder rate at a record high and firebombings day and night, business in Macau was bad. I knew it was really bad because there were more waiters than customers in the restaurant we visited the night before, and we could catch a taxi during rush hour when it was raining. Another telltale sign of the poor economy was the slew of gold-jewelry stores popping up around town. It is a paradox that citizens, including triad members, buy more gold whenever society becomes chaotic and unstable.

The turf war spilled into the streets. Rooms in hotels were empty, but their lobbies were inhabited by roughnecks hanging around and whispering on their mobile phones. They eyed the hotel entrance for every new entrant, while they chain-smoked. Cars by the roadside were burned. Explosions inside triad-controlled businesses were reported daily. Even a few policemen were murdered. Tourist visits were down to almost zero. No one in their right mind would want to visit Macau during that time.

My wife and I did. Why?

Because my wife was nuts; she wanted to be a paparazzo to the triads.

We went for one weekend during that period and it was the longest month I spent in the Portuguese enclave.

My wife got what she wanted. We ran into some triad members in front of the hotel where we were staying.

You could always tell what they were by their appearance. The older ones had Kim Jong Il hair, held in place by industrial-strength hairspray. The younger ones had greasy hair, long in the back and short on the sides. They wore casual clothes. I had yet to see one with a tie. But most of all, they wore a lot of gold – bracelets, necklaces, rings, and watches – which could easily be converted into cash in case they needed to migrate in a hurry.

They were standing around a new Mercedes. My wife urged me to stand next to them so that she could use me as a decoy as she took photos of them – an old cloak and dagger trick.

I was reluctant, because the last time I was close to such violent people was in grade two, when I had to sit next to Big Sally the class bully who was twice my size. But I did not want my wife to think I was a coward, so I gingerly moved to within a few feet of their white Mercedes. Luckily, they appeared not to notice the photo snapping because the flash did not work.

"Did the flash go off?" my wife asked.

I told her it most certainly did, and ushered her into the hotel bar. I urgently needed a drink.

Inside the bar, there were only a few customers. No one was smiling. Everyone, including the bartender, seemed to be on the lookout for something bad happening. I took a seat facing the entrance with my back against the wall. A siren was approaching, and all of us looked out the windows. All breathed a sigh of relief when the police car continued on its journey to somewhere further away.

Then suddenly there was a loud pop from inside the hotel. Everyone in the bar dove for cover. The space under our table was the nearest cover for us, and I beat my wife to it.

Happily, the bang came from the cork of a bottle of sparkling wine. But I'd had enough excitement for one day. We hurried back to Hong Kong on the next available ferry.

Thank heavens I lived to tell the story.

25

MONEY, LIES AND RELIGIONS

I am not a fan of Indonesia. Historically, the natives there were always hostile towards the Chinese. We've been to other Far Eastern countries dozens of times each, and this would be my first visit to Indonesia. I am going because my wife makes me.

I've pleaded with my wife repeatedly that it isn't a good idea to travel to Indonesia in the current political climate. But she insists on it, saying that it is the perfect time for her to do Christmas shopping there. Besides, she claims, we are only going to Bali, where no violence against Chinese people has been reported.

That's easy for her to say, since she is not Chinese. Some wife she is – willing to risk her husband's life for the sake of bargain hunting.

When the plane is already in the air, an idea strikes me. Remember those Muslims who pretended they were Chinese so that they could feast in Chinese restaurants during Ramadan? For good measure, they even brought along Chinese newspapers to read while they were eating.

What if I introduce myself as an Indonesian of Islamic persuasion? Who would know? So when my wife tries to pacify me and says: "If worst comes to worst, we can seek help from the Canadian embassy", I proudly announce my brilliant plan and add: "My name is Mohammed and I am from Bali. What is this 'we' thing you are talking about?"

"Almost everyone in Bali is Hindu, didn't you know?"

Now she tells me. I snatch the Bali guidebook from her and flip through the pages, frantically looking for a Balinese name. I settle on one I can easily pronounce: Kurut.

My wife asks: "Is that not the name of a town?" Well, it will do for now. I can't be too choosy; the plane is about to land.

Our driver is here to take us to the hotel. He looks mean and is big for an Indonesian.

He asks: "Vacationing here?"

My wife replies: "And shopping."

I add: "And visiting relatives."

He is curious as to where my relatives live. My wife pre-empts me by saying: "He is only kidding."

There goes my cover.

Now that my cover is blown, I just hope no one will bring up sensitive questions about the economy. But my wife just won't shut up. Our driver is bitter about everything and everyone, especially the hotel business and the people who work in it. He launches into a diatribe about how they make ten times the money he is making and work only eight hours a day, not to mention the tips they make on the side. My big-mouth wife continues to egg him on, asking him why he isn't working for the hotels then. Apparently, one needs to offer a bribe to get hired, and he doesn't have the money to do that.

He glances at me in the rear-view mirror and asks: "What do you do for a living?" I am glad to have the opportunity to exonerate myself. I tell him I am a writer, and I am paid close to nothing.

I am eager to change the subject, so I ask: "Whatever happened to the Suharto family?"

We are almost at the hotel now. How much should I tip him? Too little and he'll think of me as another Chinese miser; too much and he'll wonder how I got all the money.

I nudge my wife and whisper: "Please take care of the tipping, so that we don't get blamed for the volcano erupting and the forest fires as well."

My wife, whose nickname is Catty, walks out on me, saying: "My name is Cathy and I am from Canada. What is this 'we' thing you are talking about?"

PART VI

Culture Shock

26

MADE IN USA

I am a very private person. The Americans are extreme extroverts. We get along fine.

You sit down at a bar next to an American stranger and sooner or later, he will strike up a conversation with you, and before he finishes his second Budweiser, he has already told you his life story. And now he wants to hear yours.

My first meal on US soil was at a Los Angeles diner. The waitress was a tall, buxom woman with a pretty face and an easy smile. She asked: "Honey, what can I get ya?"

I was a lot younger then, and thought it was love at first sight. While I was checking my hair in the reflection from a spoon, another man walked in, and she said the same darn thing.

Same with the next 10 guys.

Talk about culture shock.

You don't comment on a Brit's accent. He will be terribly offended and retort: "I don't have an accent." I've become smarter now and say: "You talk the same way the Queen does." In the US, everyone is supposed to have an accent, including the Queen of England. When they talk to me, they can never resist asking where I'm from.

When they find out I am from Hong Kong, they say cute things like: "Wow, I love driving my Honda," or, "That Mount Fuji is awesome, man."

They love being asked about their own accents as well. It gives them a chance to tell their life stories. "I have a totally screwed-up accent. I was born in Oklahoma, but my father got transferred to New Jersey when I was three. Then when I turned four, we moved to Philly. That's when I got my first bike, after I got better from chicken pox... " And off we go again.

There are some minor disadvantages to being extroverts. One of them is that they tend to expose their ignorance readily. Generally speaking, Americans don't have a clue as to what goes on in the rest of the world; and they watch too much television.

I have a few anecdotes about Americans' concept of international monetary affairs.

I once told an American nurse from Philadelphia about the plight of people in Mainland China, and that most people there earned less than US$100 a month. She wanted to know, in earnest, why the Chinese Government could not print more money and give everyone there a bundle of it. Bless her.

Once in Denver, I asked to pay a bill with traveler's checks. The saleswoman, right on cue as if in a TV commercial, replied: "Only if it's American Express."

It took me much time and effort to convince her that Standard Chartered traveler's checks were just as good, even though you never see them advertised on US TV.

Another time, a New Orleans bartender asked me what the exchange rate was to the Hong Kong dollar. I told him one US dollar was worth about eight Hong Kong dollars. He felt so sorry for me that he bought me a drink. Imagine how much more sorry he would have felt for Sony's chairman if he had known US$1 could buy 100 yen.

These are the citizens of the most powerful nation on Earth. A country which has produced more Nobel Prize winners in recent years than all other countries combined, has the best academic institutions, and is the most advanced in medicine, science, and technology.

How did they do it?

27

WET MARKET DEBATE

The Cantonese describe a loud, chaotic and irrational altercation as "a quarrel between female hawkers". Female hawkers in wet markets are renowned for quarrels characterized by simultaneous screaming from both sides – each says what she wants and neither listens to the other.

The other day I was reminded of the market scene. The venue was a political forum organized by a TV channel. The players were Legco candidates. There were several parties going for the same few seats in one particular geographic region. Each party had three or four candidates, all dressed in different brightly colored clothing, reminiscent of the uniforms of football teams.

It has been a difficult election year for the politicians. Now the British government has gone, there is no one to kick around anymore. The safest way for a politician to win votes is to launch personal attacks on other politicians, providing a lot of entertainment for TV audiences in the meantime.

Sparks started to fly when it was time for questions and answers. Each party had to take a turn at being grilled by the other parties.

They all began with a derogatory remark: "You have a reputation for swaying like a willow in the wind," or, "You have sat on the fence for so long even your hair is parted in the middle."

The questions were more like accusations: "You voted yes on the import of foreign laborers bill, can you still sleep at night?" or "When will you start caring for the poor and grassroots citizens?"

The spokesman of one party being grilled was an old hand in politics. It did not matter what was said or asked, he calmly and stoically recited the party line. The recital – which started almost at the same time as each question and interfered with the interrogator's verbal onslaught throughout – served well to deflect the accusations and avoid the questions.

The opposition party screamed: "Answer: yes or no." He never did. He was too busy taking a stand on other issues.

The spokesperson for another high-profile party was a smart cookie. Her tactics worked to a tee. First she ignored the questions by looking elsewhere. The interrogator lost her patience and again bombarded her with a barrage of accusatory rhetoric.

Then she spoke: "You go on."

Falling into her trap, her tormentor continued to speak. It was then she drowned out her tormentor's voice by screaming: "This is so typical of your party, only you can say anything, nobody else is allowed to."

She looked around to solicit approval from other politicians. She might have gained some sympathy votes from voters too, while deftly sidestepping all the tough questions and playing the victim at the same time. In parting, she took a swipe at the spokesperson of another party by saying: "At least I didn't waste any of your time by talking gibberish like he did."

I do hope they continue to use these female hawker tactics. If they behave more like male hawkers, we will see fist fights. There are enough of those in Taiwanese politics.

28

LARRY'S HAIRY MOLES

I grew up with a guy named Larry, who was known for only one thing: He had two big moles – one at the center of his forehead, and the other on his nose. His nickname was … yes, you guessed it.

When we were in kindergarten, he cried a lot because the other children teased him about the moles. But instead of going to a doctor, his mother took him to a fortune-teller. The fortune-teller told his mother never to remove the two moles. The one on his forehead would bless him with wisdom, and the one on his nose would empower him to smell trouble – for as long as he lived.

So he was stuck with the two moles.

As he grew, they grew with him; each reaching the size of an olive. At puberty, they (both Larry and the moles) started to grow hair. Another fortune-teller told his mother never to tamper with the hair on the moles, either.

Throughout high school and university, the yearbooks consistently described him as the one least likely to commit a crime in public (imagine him in a police line-up).

Interestingly, if you were around him long and often enough, you stopped noticing the moles. That could explain why, for all those years, he had never seriously considered going against his mother's wishes and removing them.

He became a teacher after university, and you can imagine all the smirking and sniggering in his classroom, especially on the first day of school.

Whenever he met his ex-students, on the street or socially, they always mistakenly addressed him as Mr. Mak (Mak is Cantonese for mole).

In spite of the hardship brought about by the hairy moles, Larry had a good life – that is, until recently.

Happily married to a lovely woman, with two bright children, he was financially secure when he decided to take early retirement and emigrate to Canada.

Then all hell broke loose.

Everyone advised him to rid himself of the moles. They had him believe there were immigration laws prohibiting a person with that kind of "deformity" from entering North America; or that he risked promoting anti-immigration sentiments, perhaps provoking skinheads to protest, chanting things like: "No More Moles".

Mothers would possibly be inclined to shield their young children's eyes with him around. Moreover, he would be unemployable, unless he was willing to join a circus.

He finally relented, mainly because his mother was not around anymore. He went to a surgeon and had the moles removed.

The only problem now was that he bore no resemblance to the photos he had submitted earlier on with his immigration papers. Because of that, there were delays in the immigration process, followed by medical reports and affidavits, and then further delays.

When the immigration papers finally came through, property and stock prices had plummeted, and he had to sell his properties and stocks at rock-bottom prices. He started a business in Canada, but it failed. Now that he is not financially secure anymore, he has returned to Hong Kong to look for a job.

He cannot get his old job back, and cannot find a new one. He is a miserable person nowadays.

If his mother were alive, she would have said: "See, you should have listened to the fortune-tellers."

29

BARGAIN

A friend from Canada is here to visit, and she wants to do some serious shopping.

So we plan a trip down the Golden Mile – that stretch of shops on and about Nathan Road, starting from the Star Ferry terminal, all the way to Mongkok and beyond, where you can find just about everything from antiques to zebra skin.

I bring along my aunt, one of the top "price negotiators" this side of the Equator. She has a good track record. For years in the past, this woman was able to feed her family of six for a few bucks a day. She bought a nice flat with $50,000 and invested in Hongkong Bank stocks when they were under ten dollars a share. Even today, aged 67, she still has the knack of getting basement prices from the toughest vendors.

My friend Sheila is interested in some silk scarves, and is saying rather loudly how beautiful they are when my aunt stops her: "Shhh! Don't say anything." To the vendor, she says: "Where do you get these awful looking scarves from, China? The colors are all wrong, the patterns are so old-fashioned, and the sewing and cutting are of such bad quality." Then in the same breath, she asks: "How much are they, if we want to buy more than one?"

Sheila does not understand it, and protests mildly in the background that the scarves are not that bad. My aunt puts a hand over Sheila's mouth and pushes her face away. Sheila is pushed off the pavement and almost run over by the traffic. I pull Sheila back to the pavement, and tell her to let my aunt do all the talking.

It works. Sheila gets three scarves for the original asking price for one.

According to my aunt, you cannot show too much interest in the merchandise, and you must always threaten to move on and do business with someone else.

At a stall in Temple Street, Sheila is checking some bric-a-brac which she wants for her boss as a present.

My aunt sneers: "You don't have room for that kind of trash." Then turning to the vendor, she asks: "How much is this trash anyway?"

The vendor tells us the price is $120. My aunt screams: "What? You must be joking." The expression on her face is one of total disbelief.

"The stall at the corner tried to sell us the same thing for $80, and we thought that price was outrageous."

Sheila knows that's not true, but knows to keep her mouth shut.

"Let's go," my aunt orders and pushes Sheila along. About 10 meters away, she turns and yells "How about $70?"

Eventually, the deal is settled at $90.

"I'll buy it from you even though the other stall is cheaper, because you seem like a nicer man," my aunt explains to the vendor.

Sheila is also schooled in some doctrines of shopping in Hong Kong. Never hand over the money until you have checked the merchandise and have it in your hand. Labels are meaningless; check the content. Pay attention to the popular con man's adage: If a deal looks too good to be true, it probably is. An enticing sign advertising a genuine leather handbag for $20 probably means you get only the buckle for that price. There is no such thing as a refund from the street vendors.

At the end of a day of hard bargaining, Sheila and I decide to go to Lan Kwai Fong to have some fun.

My aunt declines the invitation.

"Paying a hundred dollars for a beer is no fun. I'm going home to catch a TV program about Hong Kong stocks and have fun seeing which stocks went up and which went down today," she says, before hopping on the minibus.

30

WESTERN MEDICINE IN CHINESE

During my specialist training in the United States in the 1970s, my competency in practicing Western medicine was constantly suspect because I graduated from a medical school in the Orient.

Such professional prejudice was widespread and understandable given that I was a foreigner in a country with claims of being the most advanced in medicine, science, and technology.

I must admit that in those days, being a medical graduate from the University of Hong Kong was more a hang-up for me than a source of pride.

I would have to defensively explain our curriculum, and brag about the fact that our pass rate for the notoriously condescending examination – required of all foreign medical graduates before acceptance into US training programs – was the highest in the world.

I wondered if things might have been easier for me had our medical school been named the McFadzean School of Medicine. (Alexander McFadzean was the formidable Professor of Medicine in my day). A Scottish moniker would have reflected the true nature of our education, since most of the senior teaching faculty members were from the United Kingdom.

Recently, top academics at Hong Kong University renamed the medical school for Li Ka-shing, after Mr. Li promised to donate HK$1 billion to the University's medical faculty. The reasons given were weak. They included the need for donated money to sustain medical research, the need to thank Mr. Li for his largesse, and the fact that many other medical schools in the US did the same for their most generous donors.

No one is denying that money is important for medical research, and that gratitude is owed to Mr. Li. But the issue here is whether changing the name of the medical school is the appropriate thing to do. Citing precedents in the US is a lame way of justifying the action, because American culture is different, and a medical school with an American's name attached to it carries no negative connotations, unlike a Chinese name for a school which teaches Western medicine.

Many alumni of the Hong Kong University medical school cried foul at the faculty members' decision. "The name of the medical school is not for sale," they said.

Strong and diverse opinions opposing the name change gathered steam, culminating in a decision by the Hong Kong Medical Association – the powerful doctors' union – to conduct a survey on the issue, and results showed most members objected to the name change.

No doubt, emotion prevailed over reason in such matters, but one sound argument I heard is that naming the school after Li Ka-shing probably shuts the door to other potential donors in future.

My own feeling towards the name change is that it does not add cachet to the school. In fact, it may even have the opposite effect.

Now, Li Ka-shing is as Chinese a name as it gets. A medical school with this label will give outsiders, not familiar with our education system, the impression that this is a medical school with Chinese-medicine characteristics. That is misleading because we practice Western medicine exclusively.

If I had to do specialist training in the US all over again, and had to tell US doctors that I graduated from the Li Ka-shing School of Medicine, their most likely response would be: "Who is this Li Ka-shing? Do they teach Chinese medicine there?"

The whole controversy boiled down to this: The dons at Hong Kong University received an astronomical donation from Mr. Li, and they were so overwhelmed with gratitude that they acted too hastily in renaming the medical school after him. Meanwhile, the feelings of many alumni were hurt because they were never consulted.

After all, the name of the school belongs to all medical graduates, past, present and future. The academics who called the shots and changed the name only worked there temporarily. They didn't own the school, and should have no naming rights.

PART VII

FOR YOUR HEALTH

31

ANCIENT CHINESE SECRET

I don't mean to brag. A few years ago, I could have been a doctor of traditional medicine any time I wanted.

But then, so could a lot of other people.

Until recently, when the law required a license for someone to call himself a certified Chinese doctor, the only legal requirement for practising traditional medicine was that the person had to be an ethnic Chinese.

This outdated decree was based on the assumption that one had to be Chinese to understand Chinese medicine – a profession based not on science but on a fusion of tradition, philosophy and belief.

For instance, the Cantonese have a name for the all-encompassing and nebulous condition – with symptoms that range from halitosis and constipation to acne and coughing – *yeh hei* (literally, hot air). The remedy is a herbal concoction known as *leung tsa* (literally, cool tea) – the ultimate yin-yang theory of disease and cure.

Abstinance from certain food is a mainstay of any therapeutic regimen in Chinese medicine. For *yeh hei,* the dietary advice is to stop eating fried food. Such advice epitomizes traditional Chinese medicine in being short on science but long on pragmatism. It has never been proven that fried food can cause *yeh hei*, but it really doesn't matter – eating less fried food is good for your health, regardless.

Chinese folk medicine gives new meaning to the saying "You are what you eat." For instance: Chicken feet were recommended for sprained ankles; livers from all kinds of animals for purported liver problems; pig's kidneys for kidney "weaknesses"; and so on and so forth.

Some practices are warped. Virility is a big deal to Chinese men (men in general, I suppose); hence, male reproductive organs from wild animals perceived to be virile, such as rhinos, tigers and bears, are much sought after as aphrodisiacs. Snake is as well, and is much cheaper.

There used to be a backstreet lane around Temple Street where you could find vendors selling fresh snake blood mixed with beer. Just for show, the vendors bit the heads off the snakes before they drained their blood in front of the crowd to show off their derring-do. Young men waited in line to buy the love potion, and drank it in one go in front of an appreciative audience, before swaggering off to a bordello next door.

Chinese medicine works, I'm sure, for both disease and virility, otherwise there wouldn't be so many of us on this planet. The biggest problem is – how do you tell a guru from a quack?

When I was a child, my barber decided to hang up his clippers and combs one day, change his barber shop into a clinic, and call himself a doctor. He claimed that he had inherited an ancestral medicine book with hundreds of secret herbal recipes for curing all kinds of diseases.

He even sold a lotion for curing baldness, allegedly made according to a secret formula invented by his grandfather. He displayed "before" and "after" photos in the window of his clinic.

Even at that young age, I found the photos deceiving. In the "before" photo, the man with frontal balding had his hair combed from front to back, and in the "after" photo, from back to front.

Besides, the man in both photos was wearing the same dirty shirt.

32

HEALTH AND WEALTH

The Chinese saying "Wealth weakens the body" explains why, growing up in the 1960s, I had never heard of healthy people going for a medical check-up; while in today's wealthy Hong Kong, health checks are common practice.

It should be a good thing, too. Instead of depending on healthcare professionals to fix the problem when something goes wrong, one should take charge of one's own body. That is why I went for one last month.

At Dr. Chin's clinic, as soon as he found out what I went to him for, he asked me if I carried any health insurance. After I showed him my insurance policy, he recommended that I should check into a private hospital, because my plan covered only inpatient treatments. I said I didn't have any symptoms or complaints. He asked if I ever became short of breath when I ran after a bus or a taxi, and if I felt tight in my chest afterwards. I thought for a moment and responded in the affirmative. He winked at me and told me that would do.

Before I entered the hospital as scheduled, Dr. Chin advised me to have a battery of blood tests done at the clinical laboratory two floors down from his clinic; and also an electrocardiogram and ultrasound of my abdomen while I was there.

I had a thorough physical examination while I was in the hospital, and was discharged after an overnight stay. Dr. Chin told me I was as fit as a horse.

My insurance company reimbursed me for the thousands of dollars worth of tests, and the doctor and hospital bills. My agent warned me, though, my insurance premium might be raised next year because of the claims.

Because of this one-off health check, I have learned a bitter lesson from my agent about the healthcare business in this town.

He told me the reason why the blood tests were so expensive was because my doctor took "kickbacks" of up to 40 per cent from the laboratory. And, did I know, the clinical laboratory where I went to have all the tests done – including the electrocardiogram and the ultrasound – was partly owned by Dr. Chin? I asked why he didn't mention it to me. My agent said that would be a common ethical practice by Western standards, but in the local medical community, full disclosure of doctors' business interests to their patients was almost unheard of.

All said and done, I figure Dr. Chin has benefited much more than me in numerous ways. First, I have aided and abetted him in ripping off the insurance company. He receives a huge kickback from the private laboratory – an enterprise he is part owner of.

And, at the end of the business year, he will probably receive a share of the profit, plus bonus, from the clinical laboratory.

The lesson I've learned from having a physical check-up is that to find out the status of my health, I must first enhance Dr. Chin's wealth.

33

A ROCK AND A HARD PLACE

In many ways, life was easier when I was a child. Our neighbor Mr. Chan used to say: "I don't have time to get sick." Good old Mr. Chan never took a day of sick leave in his life, and worked until the day he died.

Nowadays, Hong Kong people are more affluent, and hence more health-conscious. As the Chinese saying goes: "More money; more medical problems." When you do not have to worry about a roof over your head and food on the table, you will worry about not living long enough to enjoy life.

I am lucky in that I have never had any serious medical problems, probably because I have never had any serious money. But I do worry that, with my aging body, something potentially serious may happen to me.

I have decided to make full use of the public healthcare system. Why not? I have been a taxpayer for decades.

I know the waiting time in our public healthcare system is legendary; but it's either that or pay big bucks to seek private healthcare.

Last year, I went to a private doctor for a physical, and though the check-up was satisfactory, I was sick to my stomach when I found out he grew richer by exploiting the healthcare system, and I grew poorer because my insurance company jacked up my premium because of the claims I made after that check-up.

Now that I am retired, I have – to paraphrase our old neighbor Mr. Chan – "time to get sick".

Aging people tend to be afflicted by cataracts, so I decide to check my eyes first, in case I go blind before I can take care of the rest of my body.

Before I can be seen by a specialist ophthalmologist, I need a referral letter from a GP. That's fine. I have all the time in the world. I join a queue at a neighborhood government clinic at 6pm and get a chit, for $37, after a 30-minute wait. To see the doctor will be another hour or two of waiting. The sign outside the clinic indicates that evening clinic hours are from 6-10pm. So why not go grocery shopping first and come back at around 9:45pm?

The clinic is empty when I return. The amah gives me dirty looks because she is eager to lock up, and the doctor – who is to be the last doctor to leave the clinic, because of me – looks tired and unemotional.

I apologise for being late, and at the same time look at the clock on the wall in mild protest of the fact that I am not really late. Without looking up, he asks what is wrong with me. I reply that I need a referral letter for possible cataracts. He says he can do that for me in no time and there is no need for me to sit down, put down my shopping, or take off my overcoat. Sure enough, mission accomplished before I can finish glancing through his logbook where he has recorded all his cases for the evening. I notice that I am the last, and the 80th. No wonder he is uninterested in examining my eyes. He has already seen 79 patients in less than four hours.

It turns out the referral letter, for which I have spent $37 and a few hours' waiting time, is only an introduction letter to a specialty clinic in the eye hospital. I register at the eye clinic, get a chit and wait for an hour or so before I get to see a nurse. My destiny is now in the hands of the appointment nurse who reads the letter and decides it is not an emergency.

I complain to her that it is an emergency – in my eyes anyway.

She asks: "How long have you had this problem?"

"Two months," I lie.

She says: "See, you should have come here two months ago."

I promise her that next time I plan to see a doctor, I will book an appointment with her a year ahead, even before I know I will need one, so that I can see a doctor before I die.

It turns out, a year in advance is still not far-sighted enough.

She gives me an appointment to see an eye specialist in three-and-a-half years.

34

DOC'S BEST FRIEND

I need to consult a private GP. But it is so hard to know who to go to, because they don't advertise. So I call up a buddy – a drugs salesman who knows all the GPs in town – and ask him for help.

When I ask him why doctors in Hong Kong are such a modest bunch, he laughs so hard he almost has a heart attack. After he has stopped laughing, he tells me it is the law, and not modesty that stops doctors here from advertising. He sends me to a doctor whose clinic is close to my office. Before he hangs up, he says with a chuckle: "This Dr. Li is real modest – just look at what he hangs on the walls of his waiting room."

There are numerous mirrors on the walls. One reads: "Born Again Wah Tor." (Wah Tor was the legendary ancient healer known to bring patients back from the brink of death). Another reads: "A kind heart in a kind trade." Yet another one reads: "A medical genius." They are all gifts from friends and relatives, so it is not self-advertising.

The largest frame on the wall does not contain a mirror, but displays some Chinese calligraphy written in a script easily mistaken for an obituary: "XX Li was a bright child. He went to the best schools in Hong Kong and was particularly good in science subjects. His character is perfect, and he is a genius, etc." Someone else wrote it, not him. So it's not against the law.

Also hung on the wall is his secondary school certificate. Waaah! He scored distinctions in Chinese, geography and mathematics.

I am not the only one interested in the walls. Two older women are also touring them. I overhear one giving a running commentary of Dr. Li's career highlights: He was able to overcome all odds to get into medical school; he has saved numerous patients with end-stage diseases; he compromises his own health so that his patients can stay healthy, and so on.

Who is this woman with the motor mouth?

It's his mother.

By the time I sit down, Mom is working on another patient, telling him how lucky he is to come to the best doctor in the neighborhood. She says: "No wonder you are still sick; you have been seeing that Dr. Chan down the block."

It is my turn to see Dr. Genius. He says I have bronchitis. The diagnosis is a firm one, even without the benefit of the examination table or listening to my full medical history and all my complaints. Is he a genius or what?

I receive five medications – two liquids and three pills. I am curious as to why one of the liquid medicines has two colors – pink on the top and to one side, and the rest yellow. Another patient has already entered the examination room and I hate to disturb a genius at work, so I ask Mom. She confides in me: "We sometimes mix two types of medicine in the same bottle so that Dr. Chan cannot tell what we give to our patients. Otherwise he copies us."

While I am parting with my hard-earned money, I hear Mom raising her voice and chiding an old man. The old man protests: "But I have had this lump in my thigh for 23 years, it causes me no trouble."

Mom is mad. "You know more about medicine than my son?" she shouts, while pointing to the secondary school certificate on the wall.

If it is illegal for a Hong Kong doctor to advertise, he can always ask his mother to do it for him.

Who can blame Mom for doing it? In fact, who could blame Mom for overdoing it?

35

DON'T BUG ME

I still vividly remember the day in a New York Chinatown restaurant, many years ago, when a customer screamed bloody murder and almost fainted when a cockroach crawled across the table.

Imagine, a small thing like that.

In my experience, when people who have never had to go hungry find bugs in their restaurant food – more often than not, a Chinese eatery – they become hysterical.

They refuse to return to the restaurant, lose their appetite, and demand a refund.

This reminds me of a restaurant owner I knew in New York. Whenever a customer complained about finding a bug in their food, he would go to the table, pick up the alleged bug, put it in his mouth and chew it. After swallowing it, he would announce that the offending item was not a bug, but a black bean, or depending on the appearance of the bug, some other food item. Last I heard, he was both healthy and wealthy.

When it comes to food, I subscribe to a culture different from my Western and Westernised friends. My motto is: "Do not waste any."

I grew up finding bugs in my food. I would pick them up and throw them away, then I would check to make sure there were no more and continue shovelling food into my mouth.

As far as I am concerned, bugs in food are no big deal as long as you do not knowingly swallow them. "What is worse than finding a worm in your apple?" runs one of my children's favorite jokes. Answer: "Half a worm."

I know it is the aesthetics of it all. But scientifically, all living creatures are made up of the same constituents: protein, fat, carbohydrate, mineral and water.

Kilogram for kilogram, insects may have the same nutritional value as a T-bone steak or a lamb chop. Another fact of life is that insects are ubiquitous. Even the US Government considers a few insects in foodstuffs "normal" and acceptable for consumption.

The weirdest story about insects in food is one my children told me.

A friend of theirs was gulping down chunks of "century eggs" in steaming hot congee when a little roach crawled out from the gooey part of the egg, and scurried under the sink. It did not surprise me that the cockroach realised it could survive hot congee by using the egg yolk as a cocoon. They survived the Big Bang, the Ice Age, two world wars, and will probably survive El Nino as well.

I will not spoil your dinner by relating any more bug-in-food anecdotes, but I would like to leave the vegans out there with something to think about: How do you know that your vegan dish is strictly vegan?

PART VIII

WINE, WOMEN AND SONG

36

MY WAY

It's that time of the month again. Yes, it's when my friend JL starts calling all of us to gather at his place to make fools of ourselves.

The name of the game is karaoke. There are rules. You can bring along any companion – that is, anyone except your wife. You must drink whiskey and none of that sissy stuff like red wine or beer. Cigar smoking is highly regarded but not strictly enforced because one of the guys is 72 years old and has emphysema. And lastly, everyone can sing *My Way* only once.

I'll explain why we need the last rule. One time, I sang *My Way* and was severely criticised for not doing it right. So it followed that everyone else gave a rendition of the same song, trying to prove his was the real thing. JL was especially bad; he had a go at it at least three times. The rest of us would have continued if it had not been for the neighbors complaining to the police.

Here comes Paul. He always has three or four bimbos clinging to him like a wet towel. I don't know what he's got that I don't.

Paul and I actually have a lot in common. For example, we are the same age, and both of us still have a full set of hair on our heads.

He also has money, a partnership in a successful law firm, a nice home on the Peak, and a new Mercedes.

I have hair.

You have to give credit to those bimbos Paul has brought along. To judge them by their appearance, you might not have thought they would be intelligent enough to operate the karaoke machine. But they sure know their way around it. One of them likes to hold the two microphones close to her chest and coo: "Which one you like?"

Jerry is in the corner talking about Myanmar politics again. He is telling Bimbo A he helps the livelihood of 2,000 Burmese people by employing them in his garment factory. He is having his second whiskey. By the time he has had his fifth, the number of Burmese people he supports will undoubtedly rise to a quarter of a million.

JL is the only one I know who struts his stuff, Mick Jagger-like, singing *Unchained Melody*. For all I know, he choreographs his moves in front of a mirror before he comes to these sessions. He always insists on having a bimbo sing along with him and, when the song doesn't turn out well, he taps the bimbo on the shoulder and says: "You need practice; next time it will be better."

Three days out of the hospital, and CC is already all over Bimbo B like a rash. That old goat; if emphysema doesn't kill him, a heart attack from over-excitement probably will. I still don't believe it is necessary to wrap his arm around Bimbo B to get that special feeling for a Bee Gees number.

What is this? Bimbo C fills my glass with whiskey again? I should really slow down.

A bit of a commotion over there. Uh-oh, it's JL. He slipped and fell while trying to do a reverse moonwalk. What? He wants to do that song all over again?

James is late today. He must have had a hard time getting away from the wife. We thought we would never see him again after he got caught with a bimbo by the missus last year. You've got to give it to that guy, he is back with a vengeance. On only his second drink, he is already making a move on Bimbo D. The way he fixes his eyes on her with a soft gaze while singing *Love Me Tender*, he might as well kneel down and propose. It's so disgusting.

Bimbo C comes over and fills my glass again. She's been eyeing me the whole night. Wait till she hears me sing. I am actually a better singer than all of them, even though I don't like to sing as much as they do. Let me see, my left side is my better side, so when I go up, I should stand on the right.

Jerry, by now, is telling everyone and anyone who will listen how he single-handedly sustains the economy of Myanmar.

Who cares? It's my turn to sing, and I am going to do it my way.

37

BOYS WILL ALWAYS BE BOYS

Someone once said: "For a man to attain greatness, he must remain a boy at heart." Going by that, my friends are truly some of the greatest men alive.

One of them has started a "Friday Club" – a euphemism for a boys' night out during which we boys can smoke cigars, drink ourselves silly, and most of all, reminisce about past romances. Understandably, wives are not invited. Our leader, JL, actually goes to the trouble of faxing a flyer of the event to each household, in bold type, explaining why women are not welcome: "For your sake – because there will be too much foul language, smoke, and unruly behavior."

My wife becomes suspicious only after seeing the flyer. She asks: "You boys behave like that all the time, so why are you being so considerate of us all of a sudden?"

I wonder if this gathering is going to be as boring as the "Karaoke Club" JL organized a few months ago. Not that they have anything new to tell. Paul Lee will brag about his adventures in France while he was working in Europe. For someone who admits he lost his virginity at the ripe age of 32, on the night of his wedding, he sure has been making up for lost time and chasing everything in a skirt. Jerry Pang's hunting ground was Myanmar, where he used to own factories. It you believe only half the stories he tells of his past love interests there, he could not possibly have held down a full-time job. JL is getting on in age now, but he loves to tell us how ladies in Taiwan used to weep non-stop when seeing him off at the airport.

I am the last one to arrive at the rendezvous. Jerry and Paul are in the middle of a heated argument. JL tells me they are fighting over a manhood-enlargement pill. Apparently Paul is able to procure the pill through the internet, and according to him, it is fast-acting, long-lasting, and clinically proven.

I'll be darned. I would love to have that.

Paul has brought it along to show off, but Jerry snatches it from him and claims ownership. Before he puts it in his back pocket, he licks it to deter Paul from claiming it back.

Paul is pleading with Jerry now, with tears in his eyes. Jerry says no way will he return it, and that Paul still owes him a few CDs, borrowed a year ago. Besides, he really, really needs that pill.

Desperation drives Paul to violence. He ambushes Jerry and forces his hand into Jerry's back pocket. Pulling at each other's clothing, they fall to the floor. While they wrestle, that little pill pops out and rolls towards me.

I cannot believe my luck. I casually drop a napkin to the floor near my feet and pick the pill up together with the napkin. After covering my nervousness by pretending to sneeze, I stealthily put the pill into my shirt pocket.

Jerry and Paul have stopped wrestling now and are blaming each other for the loss of the pill. I help them look for it too – most diligently. Paul accuses Jerry of hiding it somewhere close to his body, so Jerry takes all his clothes off to prove his innocence. We decide not to let him put his clothes on again – if he is treacherous enough to have swallowed the pill during the commotion, the incremental effect on his manhood will be proof enough.

After an hour, we acquit him through lack of evidence and let him put his clothes back on.

I am so happy I have the pill in my possession. When I return home, my wife asks: "What kind of mischief have you got yourself into now?" I say none. "Then how come you have that stupid smile on your face?" she says, before she slams the bedroom door.

Well, I am so excited about that pill I may not be able to sleep anyway. I'd sure like to try it; but not tonight, when I'm sleeping alone on the sofa.

38

BAD AFTERTASTE

I almost died at a wine-tasting party – not from drinking, but from embarrassment. I made the mistake of bringing Willie along.

It all started when I told my wine merchant friend that in spite of all the economic success, and years of exposure to Western culture, many of my compatriots still mix good wine with soda pop.

It would be fine if the wine used was plonk, but in order to give face, sometimes they use Petrus or Lafite.

My friend, the wine aficionado, almost choked on his cabernet sauvignon, and said that a little wine education for my compatriots in China would fix that. Incidentally, he was hosting a wine-tasting session and my compatriots and I could come and learn something.

I asked whether I could bring all 1.3 billion but he said to pick one. And of the 1.3 billion, I had the misfortune of picking Willie.

I like Willie. He is a fun guy, but callous, uncouth and rowdy. Now I also know that he cannot hold his liquor. I am no expert, but I figured that I knew a little more about wine tasting than Willie, so I gave him a crash course. I sensed that we could be in for a long night when I found out that Willie could not accept having to spit out the wine after tasting it.

"I thought we were invited for a few free drinks," he said.

I introduced him to the technique of exposing the wine to all parts of the palate in order to appreciate the fine art of wine-making. He nodded knowingly, and said: "Like using mouthwash, right?"

Even while we were on the first bottle, I caught Willie cheating. I noticed that what came out of his mouth after tasting was only a fraction of what he had taken in. By the time we got to the third bottle, Willie's face was beefy red and he started to tilt his head back when he was tasting his wine. Easier for him to swallow, I guess.

Then he smacked his lips and let out an "Arrrrh" before he spat into the bucket. And as everyone else was gently spitting out the wine, Willie was spitting, period.

He was totally wasted by the time we got to the seventh bottle. He was loud and pushy, and was shaking everybody's hand and thanking them for the good wine and good time.

I tried to distance myself from him, but this was quite impossible because he came over every five minutes to put his fat arm around my neck, displaying camaraderie for the whole world to see.

I did not dare look anybody in the eye for the rest of the evening, and left with Willie (with said arm around my neck), without saying goodbye to anyone.

On the way home, Willie said: "Let's do it again."

I said: "Over my dead body."

39

MASSAGING THE EGO

Call me strange, but I don't enjoy going to massage parlors. Whenever my friends are all gung-ho about visiting one for a massage, I always beg off. But sometimes they insist that I go with them, telling me that loyalty to friends is of paramount importance. What can I do? I am the last person in the world to be a party pooper.

I can see why a lot of men like going to massage parlors. No matter who you are and what you do for a living, the moment you step inside the joint, they make you feel like a tycoon. It is an ego trip.

The maitre d' bows to us and coos: "This way please, big bosses." We follow her, swaggering along and enjoying our newfound status.

We are sharing a big room – except for JP, who is ushered into a private room because he wants some "extra service" today.

Before long, we are all lying down buck-naked under towels, waiting to be waited on. Personally, I feel more secure in public with my clothes on and in an upright position.

We each get our own masseuse. Soon the whole room is filled with kimono-clad women. With my face down, lying on a massage stretcher, all I can see are bare legs milling around.

On principle, I don't ever want a stranger to mess with my body. But for the sake of loyalty to friends, I'll take a chance this time.

When they are finished with our backs, we have to turn over to have the front of the body worked on. That maneuver is a little hard for CK, whose mind apparently has wandered off into impure thoughts while his body is being relieved of stress and strain.

When all is done, we drag our sore bodies to the sauna. I wish CK would stop steaming up the room by constantly pouring water over the furnace. I just can't see the appeal of the sauna for someone like CK. He doesn't do any sport, refuses to help his wife with any housework, and never takes any public transportation without air conditioning. In other words, he doesn't like to sweat.

Now we are supposed to jump into a pool filled with ice-cold water. I am not keen on this hot-cold treatment, for the same reason I am not into self-flagellation. Before they can accuse me of disloyalty, I make it clear that I am avoiding the pool because I would rather not share the same bath water with JP. You never know where he's been.

The bathroom attendant is too obsequious for my liking. First of all, I am not Mr. Big and I don't deserve to be treated like one.

Secondly, I am not about to pay big bucks to have my toenails clipped. I can do that very well myself, thank you.

Stepping out of the parlor is like going back to the future. No one is going to call us big boss, or wait on us hand and foot anymore. The endorphin effect is wearing off fast but the muscle aches still linger on.

CK says: "I feel much lighter now."

Sure, $1,000 lighter.

40

ELVIS IS EVERYWHERE

Our government officials are constantly pushing for Hong Kong to become a hub for one thing or another. They can now add one more to the list – a hub for Elvis Presley impersonators.

It was the 65th birthday bash for the Founding President of the Elvis Presley Alliance of Asia. The great man is a Malaysian Chinese living in Hong Kong. A total of thirteen Elvis impersonators from all over Asia came to Hong Kong to celebrate with him. I was there, too.

By the way, nowadays they call themselves Elvis Tribute Artists (ETAs), because being called an Elvis impersonator is too demeaning, especially for Elvis.

We all gathered in a big room at a posh hotel, and were treated to an evening of Elvis music and fine wine in a high-octane showbiz atmosphere. It was great fun.

Apart from having thoroughly enjoyed myself, I also had time to make some observations.

First of all, none of the ETAs looked like Elvis. The main reason is that no matter how many cosmetics are used, it's still impossible to look like a white boy from Tupelo, Mississippi when you are Japanese, Filipino, Chinese, or Thai. The only Caucasian ETA there – a Sicilian from Australia now living in the Philippines – didn't look anything like him, either. What do I mean? When he picked up a baby in the audience, that poor infant girl burst into tears after staring at his face for a few seconds. The mother grabbed the baby back, while right on cue, another ETA started to belt out *Don't Be Cruel.*

Not that they didn't try hard enough to look like the King. They all had the Elvis ensemble: the ducktail, the sideburns, and the heavily-jeweled white jumpsuit image of Elvis from his *Aloha From Hawaii* show in 1973.

If anything, they tried too hard.

Many of them were too old to have enough hair for a quiff, so they wore wigs. But the wigs were so unnaturally stiff that when *All Shook Up* was sung, none of the hairdos were. Some glued-on sideburns were so bushy that they clogged the ear canals and made the ETA look like a *Hound Dog.* The ETA who sang *Jail House Rock* had a turned-up collar so wide and tall he could hide an AK-47 in it.

The jumpsuits were so outrageously rich in rhinestones and sequins, fringes and frills that the evening could easily have been mistaken for a Liberace lookalike contest.

The Sicilian ETA's jumpsuit was cut so low in the front I could see his belly button. That could be quite scary, especially for small children, because he was endowed with chest hair luxuriant enough for a wolverine to raise a family in there.

Everything was over the top, probably to compensate for not doing Elvis justice by looking handsome enough.

But you've got to love those guys. To become an ETA requires absolute dedication and true love for the King's music, with a heavy dose of eccentricity and a self-effacing sense of humor. It is a hobby for those guys, who all have respectable day jobs, including one who works as a highly qualified gynecologist. I am singling him out because I love the idea of his patients claiming that Elvis is their gynecologist.

Not everyone is a fan of Elvis. Earlier in his career, Jack Gould of the *New York Times* wrote: "Elvis's phrasing ... consists of stereotyped variations that go with a beginner's aria in a bathtub." Another critic in that same era, Ben Gross of the *New York Daily News*, commented: "His exhibition ... tinged with the kind of animalism that should be confined to bordellos." Both of them must have kicked themselves when Elvis became the greatest pop icon of our lifetimes.

But their points are well taken – Elvis Presley is not a tough act to follow.

That's why Elvis is everywhere.

PART IX

CAN WE TALK?

41

SWEAR BY IT

After years of research – by asking different nationals to swear in their respective languages – I have reached the conclusion that, when it comes to swearing, the Hong Kong Cantonese have no equals.

Like everything else in Cantonese, the swear words are vulgar but apt. Let me give you some examples.

While people from most countries would settle for insulting just you, a Cantonese man will say something to insult your mother instead. In saying that, it is implied that he could be your father, therefore you are a bastard and your father is a tortoise – someone who shares his wife.

Sometimes a Cantonese man can get so carried away with rage that he swears at his children the same way, until a bystander reminds him: "Hey, that's what you are supposed to do anyway."

With a few choice words, he also describes the sorry status of your mother's reproductive system, so that everyone knows that your mother has an incurable infectious disease. Why anyone would want to boast about having a liaison with a woman like that is beyond me.

Every language has a name for a guy who is no good. Depending on the situation, the English language may label him a jerk, a nerd, a doofus, a nincompoop, and you know the rest and the best. The Cantonese call him that too, except that he is also in an aroused state. That makes sense, because if most of that guy's circulation is drawn to that part of his anatomy, the brain is sure to be deprived of oxygen, hence his behavior and demeanor.

Those same words are used to describe someone who is ugly. Come to think of it, nothing can be uglier than having a face which resembles a male sexual organ in an aroused state.

Sometimes a whole family is cursed. A curse of that magnitude calls for some tact, even for the Cantonese. So you will hear something like: "Your whole family will get rich." Do not thank him yet. What he means is that you and every member of your clan will be offered the kind of money which comes in million-dollar denominations, and is burned in bundles at funeral homes.

To lend credence to a story, unlike other nationals who would swear by it in the name of their children, the Queen, or God, the Cantonese man promises you kinky sex.

To strike a deal, you or I would put up collateral or something. The Cantonese man instead promises to subject himself to humiliating sex acts – he will do this and that for you, for as many times as you want, for free. To show his sincerity, he even makes explicit gestures simultaneously so you know exactly what kind of deal you are getting into.

Enough said. If you find the above examples not compelling enough, it is probably because a lot has been lost in translation.

42

PERCEPTION IS REALITY

WK and I are about to sit down in an MTR train when a woman from the opposite bench shouts to WK: "Mr. Lai, am I glad to see you?"

The woman is Mrs. Tsui, who works as a janitor in one of the best government secondary schools in Hong Kong – where WK teaches English. With her is her 12-year-old son, who is looking for a secondary school exempted from the mother-tongue teaching scheme.

Being a career teacher, WK immediately starts lecturing Mrs. Tsui on the merits of mother-tongue teaching.

According to him, it has been scientifically proven that mother-tongue teaching improves students' knowledge and their grades. The problem with using English as the teaching medium for students whose English standard is not up to it, is that they find it hard to understand the subject matter and soon lose interest in the subject.

WK jokingly adds: "Sometimes it's not entirely the students' fault, because I have a problem understanding some of those teachers' English too."

Mrs. Tsui retorts succinctly: "If mother-tongue teaching is so good, why don't they force it on top schools like La Salle, Queen's and St Paul's Co-ed?"

WK replies: "Well, that's because these schools can demonstrate their proficiency in teaching and learning in English."

Like a good civil servant, he has an answer for everything.

I tend to agree with Mrs. Tsui, so I interject: "That's not really a reason, though. If they've done well using English as the teaching medium, shouldn't they do even better with the mother tongue?" Even WK has no answer for that one.

Mrs. Tsui wants her son to become a civil servant – secure job, good pay and a good pension.

"Look at the senior civil servants. They all speak perfect English, and that is why they've become mandarins."

WK disagrees. "They don't speak perfect English. You have that perception because you don't speak the language. Some of them try so hard to emulate their old colonial masters' accent and inflection that they sound pretentious. Now that Hong Kong is under Chinese rule, the ability to articulate perfectly in Chinese is more important than being wishy-washy in both English and Chinese."

Mrs. Tsui asks: "How many of you civil servants send your children overseas to learn English?"

WK patiently says that he thinks a lot of them have children studying overseas but they do not go overseas just to learn English, even though studying overseas is perceived as a better opportunity to learn English.

WK gives us another lecture. "English in this part of the world is more than about getting a good job; it is also about elitism," he says. "That's why so many local people like to show off their English-language skills whenever there's an opportunity. Another bad habit of many local people is the mixing of Cantonese with English, usually within the same sentence, as if their Cantonese is not good enough.

"A case in point is that annoying radio station that has DJs speaking half English and half Chinese. I wonder how much damage that radio station has done to the language ability of young people in Hong Kong."

Mrs. Tsui finally gets to her point. She wants her son in WK's school.

"I worry so much about my dumb son's English-language skills, but I don't have the money to send him overseas," she says as she puts a finger to her embarrassed son's temple and gently pushes his head away.

WK tries to convince her again there is nothing wrong with the school her son is at now, but Mrs. Tsui appears to be oblivious to his eloquent arguments.

"I want him to speak perfect English like those high-ranking civil servants, so he can get a good job."

WK shrugs and says to me: "Perception is reality." Amen.

43

NO NEWS IS GOOD NEWS

Many moons ago, we turned on the TV and watched one of the English channel's evening news programs.

My mother got so worked up watching it I almost had to take her to the emergency room.

Call me a sexist, but I believe that people making a career out of showing their faces on the TV screen should be good looking. The presenters for that day, a man and a woman, were not what I would describe as good sorts. The woman was so tiny I got the distinct impression of a little old lady behind a big steering wheel.

When she blinked, her eyelids first shut tight, then when they opened again, they seemed to overshoot the confines of the eye sockets before settling into their natural positions.

And she blinked a lot. My doctor friend tells me this could be a sign of a thyroid disease, but I am more inclined to think that it is simply a sign of a poor-fitting contact lens.

So what about the male presenter? Well, take my word for it, I am in no position to criticise anybody's looks, but my mother said that even I looked better than he did. Besides, how could anyone concentrate on what he had to say, when that bald spot on his scalp kept beaming reflected light into the living room?

"Don't be so chirpy. People are dying, for Christ's sake," my mother shouted. The woman presenter was reporting on a flood that killed dozens.

"Calm down, watch your blood pressure," I told mom, who had left the hospital only a few days before.

"I don't believe this. How can anyone muck up a word like Vietnam? Go home and practise: Vietnam, Vietnam, Vietnam, before you come out again," my mother continued. I poured her a glass of wine.

The male presenter was reporting on a world economic summit. My mother, by that time, was hysterical. She shouted: "Are we supposed to believe anything you say, when all you do is read from a script?"

I tried my best to calm her down, and explained that they were supposed to "read" the news.

She wouldn't relent. "Talk to us, instead of acting like you're still in journalism school." I refilled her glass of wine.

The man moved on to sports news. Do you know that presenters are not allowed to use the same verb twice? So we heard: beat, trampled, annihilated, crushed, destroyed, squashed, edged, drubbed, and so on. The presenter was a little embarrassed himself. My mother rolled her eyes.

It was the woman's turn again. My mother yelled: "I don't believe this, she is stumbling over another simple word." The veins on mother's forehead started to pop out and she was sweating profusely.

I said calmly to her: "They don't get paid that much, mom." My mother shouted angrily: "They shouldn't get paid at all while they're practising on us."

I threatened to turn the television off, but she wouldn't let me.

"I want to know what the weather is going to be like tomorrow, do you mind?" She was getting increasingly testy.

The weather girl managed to send her over the edge. She lost it before the girl even got to the forecast.

"Why are you whispering, you moron? It's not even cold. Relax."

I brought out the sphygmomanometer and took her blood pressure. It was critically high. She finally saw things my way and allowed me to turn the TV off.

This happened many months ago. Given the high turnover rate of TV presenters here, the ones we watched have probably skipped town by now. The current presenters, I am sure, are real pros. But someone needs to tell me first that it is safe for someone with a weak heart to watch the news.

Until then, I will not let my mother go near it again.

44

HONG KONG'S HANGUP

"Gibberish, gibberish, can I *hep choo*?" Sounds familiar? This is often the response when you make a phone call to a company in Hong Kong.

Secretaries, receptionists and telephone operators think they are too good for the job to start with. And with typical Hong Kong-style efficiency – that is, get the job done as quickly as possible at the expense of courtesy, consideration and kindness – they start talking before they put the mouthpiece to the mouth, or before they push the flashing button. They also mumble the name of the company so quickly that, as a result, you only get the *hep choo* bit.

Thinking that it is the boss's secretary, with whom you have spoken before, you ask: "Mrs. Chan?" The answer comes quickly: "Not here." Then comes the click, before you can tell the party at the other end of the line that you do not really want to talk to Mrs. Chan, but her boss, or anyone else in the company who can help you with your problem.

So you call back, wait for a few seconds before you put the phone to your ear so that you do not have to hear *hep choo* again. You are smarter now. Skip all the pleasantries, and go straight to what you want before that person hangs up again. But she is not ready for that yet. Protocol requires a few standard questions first. She asks: "What's the name?" You tell her your name. "How you spell?" You spell the whole thing for her. "What company?" No company. "Telephone?" Instead of wasting time arguing with her that it is irrelevant, you make up a number.

"What's this call pertaining to?" You need some information about their freight service and the importation of wine. You have already spoken to their boss once, and he told you to do a long list of things, but the Customs and Excise people say you still need something else, what should you do? "Oh, wrong department, I'll transfer you." Click.

"This is freight, can I …"

You speak before he can continue, to avoid hearing those two words one more time. What? He does not know what this call is about? You have just spent 15 minutes explaining your problem to his colleague. He asks: "What's your name?" You are a little annoyed now, so you say it does not matter, you just want some answers and are not interested in sharing your personal data with strangers. You take a deep breath, and explain your problem all over again. He says: "I have never dealt with this problem before, maybe you should talk to my supervisor. I'll transfer you."

Someone picks up the phone, but he is talking to someone else. You hear a distant voice talking about the soccer match on TV last night. So you wait.

He has finished talking to his office buddies now. Instead of the cheerful chatter, you hear a stern and almost hostile voice asking: "Who is this?"

You ask him whether that other person who transferred the call has told him what this call is about.

"Nope, but can I *hep choo*?"

45

THE VOICE OF HONG KONG

I was driving the other morning and, on a whim, I tuned the car radio to a talk show channel.

I was curious to hear a voice from the past. The talk show host sounded exactly like the hawker who used to sell "white sugar cake" in the neighborhood I grew up in. The voice was very distinctive in that it was both hoarse and loud. I remembered my father telling me that people had gotten that kind of voice from yelling all day long.

It is my experience that people with that kind of voice win all arguments. I still remember that year when the government imposed water rationing, because the reservoirs were drying up as a result of an unusually dry season. My father and I had to queue up to fetch water with buckets from the communal water station in the village center.

When we got to the front of the line, the hawker barged in before us. My father, who was soft-spoken, pointed out to him that he was queue-jumping and we were there first. With his booming raspy voice, the hawker yelled, for everyone within a mile to hear: "All right, you want to be first, I'll let you be first." Then he slipped in behind us. While my father was reasoning with him that it was not a matter of wanting to be first, that it was our turn to be next, and that he shouldn't have insinuated himself into second-in-line either, the hawker's booming voice drowned out my father's every word.

The hawker went into a diatribe about how everyone was always in a big rush, life was too short, and he would never fight for a small thing like that. He said all this while slowly shaking his head. To people at the back of the line, he smelled like roses. How magnanimous of him to "let" us go first, and how petty of us to fight over something like that.

The talk show host was also winning every argument. He first questioned a legislator on the phone as to why she had supported government approval of a fee increase for a public utility company. Then he delivered his own opinions on the matter with his booming voice, and the legislator could not get a word in. When the legislator finally had a chance to speak, the talk show host soon interrupted her and drowned out her explanation with another diatribe.

After a break, the host made an announcement: "Today's editorial in XYZ newspaper is total nonsense." I was holding my breath for his in-depth analysis of the issue, but it never came. He concluded by adding: "That newspaper is trash; its editorials are always worthless." They were, because he said so.

The most colorful part of that morning's show was his accusation of a government official "not wanting" and "being afraid" to appear on his TV show the other night. From what I read in the newspaper, the official couldn't make it to his show because it was short notice and the official had a previous engagement. "There is a difference between 'not able to' and 'not wanting to'," I thought.

He had no qualms about the conflict, and could not hide the glee in his voice when he talked about all the media attention he was getting. The only misgiving was when the Hong Kong Chief Executive spoke up on the matter; he didn't mention the host by name.

"Why is it that so many people dislike me?" he asked, and undoubtedly was slowly shaking his head at the same time.

I couldn't stand it anymore, so I turned the radio off.

I think our Chief Executive has the right idea. Ignore him, and he might just go away.

PART X

DEVIL IN DISGUISE

46

THE LITTLE BLUE DEVIL

The chairman of the board is smiling from ear to ear as he walks in.

The company stock has surged another five per cent in value this week, solely due to the phenomenal sale of that wonder drug. He waits for the boys to calm down from slapping each other on the back before he can get down to the serious business of making money.

He asks the chief operating officer: "What is the death toll worldwide this week?" The COO replies: "Only seven, sir. All of them were old men with pre-existing heart problems, who shouldn't have been taking the pill to start with."

The chairman smiles and says: "If this magic bullet were available years ago, these men would have been a lot fitter from having sex three times a day since their youth, and would not have croaked on us now."

The chairman continues: "That is why we should really target our sales at younger men. The authorities approve our drug as a cure for impotence, but let's not kid anyone. What man doesn't need a little help now and then? We are basically selling a performance-enhancing drug and who is going to stop us? It is not like the International Olympic Committee is looking over our shoulders and checking blood samples from our clients. What are they going to do if they find healthy men taking the drug? Ban them from having sex for life? Ha ha ha. And I have no qualms about selling the pill as a recreational drug either. The Drug Enforcement Agency can't touch us. Who can tell whether the pill is for recreation or procreation?"

The boys around the table all nod in agreement with the chairman. You don't argue with success.

The chairman wants an update on the lawsuit filed by the wife of a 70-year-old man who ran away with a young woman after having regained his manhood, thanks to the pill.

The corporate lawyer reports: "Our line of defense is going to be that our pill doesn't instigate infidelity, people instigate infidelity. We are going to pin the blame on the character flaw of that old geezer, who for years hung his head low because he could not rise to the occasion." He has overused that pun so much, no one chuckles anymore. He continues: "Now that he can perform as a man again, he doesn't want to waste his time and effort on his wife. Instead, he prefers frolicking with young waitresses down in Florida. Is that our fault?"

"Can we apportion some blame to his old lady?" someone asks. The legal eagle replies: "Definitely. We are going to blame her for her husband's impotence in the first place. Doctors have said all along: the cause of impotence in a 70-year-old man is his 69-year-old wife."

The chairman says: "While we are on the subject of lawsuits, we are going to pull out all the stops to go after those cowboys who want to capitalize on our trademark. First a perfume, then a dessert named after our pill. There is even a shop for sex toys in Hong Kong using our name. If we want an enterprise based on the name of our pill, we'll build it ourselves."

The marketing manager interjects: "We are planning to launch a wine, especially made for men, named after the pill. You know – ordinarily, alcohol increases the desire but decreases the ability. We are going to buck the trend by adding the pill to the wine, hence increasing both the desire and the ability. It's going to be a winner."

The chairman asks: "What is the progress on developing a pill that does the same thing for women?" The scientific director replies: "Nothing yet, sir. Our star scientists are still in the Bahamas wallowing in glory. With their lucrative stock options and their participation in the ongoing trials of their own invention, they are in no hurry to get back to work."

There being no other business, the chairman adjourns the meeting.

47

THANK GOD

I am not a Christian and have never been one, but Christianity did me a lot of good during my formative years.

When I was a boy, our neighbor Mrs. Chan was the quintessential pragmatic Hong Kong person. She worshiped all sorts of Buddhist gods, but became a Catholic as soon as the neighborhood church started giving out free food.

Not that it did her any good. Most times they gave her cheese which she thought was soap. She complained bitterly when it did not produce any lather. When finally told it was not soap but a dairy product called "chee-see", she gave it to me because neither she nor her son could stand the smell of it.

I loved cheese, and ate all that was thrown my way. So Christianity indirectly contributed to my well-being, even at that young age.

Mrs. Chan's son became a Catholic too. He got baptized in a hurry so that he could apply for a tuition-fee exemption in the local Catholic school.

In spite of his Catholic upbringing, he was a naughty boy. I asked him once what he told the priest in the confession booth. He said he confessed to the same sin every week – he had used foul language. I asked him why. He said it was fun because he could repeat the four-letter words in front of the priest.

I went to his church often, but only to play table tennis.

Soon they found out I spent a lot more time at the ping-pong table than in the catechism class, and I became the youngest person in Hong Kong to be banned from a church.

When I became a teenager, I started going to a Baptist church for the youth congregation. I spent many Saturday evenings there, trying to act like a responsible young adult, but secretly I was just happy to be there with the many young ladies in the group.

The best times were around Christmas, when we had to practice choir singing night and day, so that we could spread the gospel all night long on Christmas Eve – the only night of the year we could stay out overnight with parental consent. I couldn't sing to save my life, but the promise of female companionship made me overcome my lack of talent, my inhibitions, and other inadequacies.

Had they known my ulterior motive, no doubt I would have been kicked out of that church too.

Apart from the many pleasant moments singing and rubbing shoulders with members of the opposite sex, I also reaped the reward of being seen as a churchgoer. By spending a lot of time with Christians, I was kept too busy to be led astray by Mrs. Chan's son, who became a triad member later in life.

My life then was never far from Christianity. When I finished primary school, I managed to get into a famous Catholic secondary school, a stepping stone to Hong Kong University, a degree, and a guaranteed comfortable life for years to come. The Catholic school took me in, even though on my application form I had proclaimed to be an atheist.

Throughout my youthful years, I listened to a lot of sermons and became very familiar with the Bible. Armed with that knowledge, I chose a subject called *The New Testaments* for my school certificate examination, instead of the more difficult Chinese Literature and History. I did well on that subject, boosting my moderately successful academic record. Again, Christianity contributed to my well-being.

In spite of what Christianity did for me, I never became a Christian. Why not? In the words of Groucho Marx, I don't care to belong to any club that will have me as a member.

48

HELP SMOKERS, NOT HATE THEM

Smoking has been banned in all public places since 2009. But smoking continues in many bars and restaurants, especially the small and family-run ones. The battle by anti-smoking crusaders continues, and the most pressing issue on their agenda is passive smoking.

One of our health chiefs once said: "Second-hand smoking is a very polite way of forcing people to inhale carcinogens." He, of course, had carte blanche to bash smokers because they are perceived as lawless, addictive villains, and most of all, a minority in society.

Rhetoric aside, smoking in the presence of those who detest the smell and involuntarily suffer from it is indefensible. The fact that many smokers try defending it makes the situation even more offensive.

It is no wonder that anti-smoking policies are generally hostile towards smokers.

In my opinion, there is no place for outright hostility towards anyone who is addicted to anything. Although perceived as a weakness, addiction is part of human nature, and we are all prone to it. Hostility deriving from fanaticism does not win hearts or change behavior. After all, tobacco consumption is legal, and is not the only thing that is killing us slowly.

Hostility breeds hostility, and usually results in defiance and anti-social behavior. As predicted, in the ensuing years after the smoking ban in public places, smokers have continued to smoke and break the law. Enforcement has been a headache. There have been a few cases of assault on anti-smoking inspectors carrying out their duties. Smokers crowd around entrances to buildings and make pedestrians suffer smoke exposure. Cigarette butts are everywhere in places where smoking is allowed.

The ban has made smokers' lives more difficult, but has not made them quit.

The most unsavory aspect of smoking is that people usually become hooked when they are young and reckless, and it's an addiction very hard to kick.

For centuries, emperors in China tried banning tobacco use among their subjects by imposing penalties as drastic as death, but without success. This is the kind of devil we are dealing with.

I knew someone who was able to kick his heroin addiction but continued to smoke after numerous attempts to quit.

One thing is for sure. Regardless of the ban, smokers will continue to smoke, and as long as tobacco is available, new addicts will pick up the habit – a reality cogently illustrated by heroin addiction.

Perhaps there should be a change of tact in dealing with smokers. Instead of concentrating on efforts to alienate and punish tobacco addicts, society could do more to engage and help them.

The Government could orchestrate a campaign to promote responsible smoking behavior, such as abstinence in the company of people who are vulnerable or objectionable to the smoke. If all smokers were considerate of non-smokers, we would not even need a smoking ban in public places.

Another approach to think about is the use of technology to help solve the problem. For example, a hood that could trap and eliminate all the smoke would enable smokers to get their fix without having to do so in isolation.

In addition to a smoking ban in public places and a prohibitive tobacco tax, there should also be widespread government-sponsored clinics providing nicotine replacement therapy, counseling, and even hypnotherapy. Are we not doing our best to help heroin addicts in our numerous methadone clinics? Should we not show the same compassion for tobacco addicts, too?

Even Judith Mackay, the matriarch of anti-smoking crusaders, once said: "I don't hate the smokers, only the smoking."

49

IMMIGRATION BLUES

Never joke with immigration or customs officers. That was what that Thai doctor found out when he went through Hong Kong Immigration and Customs and said jokingly: "Yeah, I'm carrying drugs." He was jailed for 18 months even though (I am not making it up) they found nothing on him. When approached by the media upon his release, he said "No comment." He had learned his lesson.

I can empathize with that sentiment. Travelers tend to act goofy sometimes, probably because of the body clock thing. Still, we must always remember – never joke with those people.

I travel to Mainland China frequently. It is much easier now with my home visit card, because I can use the e-channel and never have to deal with any official. But when I had to use my foreign passport and a visa, they always found fault with my travel document, and they were trained to be immune to humor and fun. One time I joked: "I'm Chinese, too." The official threw my passport back to me and turned his back. I was in a bind. Was it a signal for me to slip a $100 bill inside my passport before I gave it back to him to examine again? And could I be arrested for bribery if I did?

My wife has a perfect solution to that dilemma. Whenever she travels to countries with a corrupt reputation, she puts a US$20 bill inside her passport by "mistake", and waits to see what happens when the immigration officer finds it. The worst that can happen to her is to apologise for being such an airhead.

When traveling to North America, take my advice, never go through the customs queue manned by a Chinese woman, especially if she looks like a new immigrant herself. She will ask tough questions. "Any fake Lolexes?" "How much cash is your six-month-old baby carrying?" "You paid only $20 for that gold chain?" She will go through all your stuff with a fine toothcomb if she has merely a hunch that you are breaking the law. I think it is a case of "it takes one to know one".

Going through customs manned by someone of Indian extraction is no picnic either. Don't be fooled by the friendly facade ("Velcome to Canada"). They too are tough and thorough. Only after you are cleared do they become friendly again, giving you patronizing advice, such as: "Go see the CN Tower. I did when I came here last year."

A few years ago, when I took a plane to Australia, the immigration officers actually disguised themselves as airline staff and sprayed us with chemicals before landing. They said that the chemicals were for getting rid of insects that might harm their agriculture. I didn't believe them and joked that I did not have body lice. They sprayed me twice.

On a more recent trip to Australia, I found that the spraying was not done any more. I dared not joke again, and quietly asked the Aussie sitting next to me about it. He told me the operation was now clandestine – they disinfected us by mixing the chemicals with the air inside the cabin.

O Lord! If those chemicals were addictive, I might have to keep going back to Australia.

50

SPEAKEASY

Last week, for the first time in my life, I was summoned to appear in court.

A few months ago, my car broke down near Hollywood Road. I looked for a mechanic but was unable to find one because it was a Saturday and a racing day. I didn't think I could find one on Sunday, either. I had no choice but to leave the car there over the weekend.

When I returned on Monday morning, I found not *one* but *four* parking tickets on the windscreen.

I thought four tickets for a single violation was unreasonable. So instead of paying the fines right away, I requested a hearing.

I arrived that morning in the magistracy to find the place rather scary. The presiding magistrate, in a black robe, sat high up on a dais, and she was as charming and warm as a card-dealer in a Macau casino – but more intimidating because she could put people in jail for contempt of court. When the names of defendants were called, they were to walk up to a microphone placed in the center of the room and answer questions.

The magistrate's microphone worked well but ours did not. With her booming voice, she would sternly order: "Speak louder." We would if only we could.

Adding to her aura, many defendants kowtowed to her and addressed her as "the Great Judge" before speaking out.

The first batch of "criminals" that morning were illegal hawkers. They all pleaded guilty, and the magistrate fined them each a few hundred dollars. One old man apparently was a regular – it was his ninth offence. All the pomp and intimidation had not deterred him from being a repeat offender.

So far, the only words that came out from her highness' mouth were: "How do you plead?"… "Fine, six hundred dollars."… and, "Speak louder."

The next batch of "criminals" were people like myself – people who had been issued parking tickets and felt betrayed by the system. No one in this group pleaded guilty (otherwise we would not have been here). The new words coming from her highness' mouth were: "Go to window three and make an appointment for another hearing."

When my name was called, I stepped forward to the microphone and told my story, looking for sympathy and understanding.

I reasoned with the magistrate that my car had broken down and I could not fix it until after the weekend, and would like to know if there were special provisions for reducing the fine in cases such as mine.

"Speak louder," she said.

I took a deep breath and repeated my plea. She responded by putting words in my mouth: "You want to plead guilty, and then you don't want to."

I protested that perhaps there should be special considerations for extenuating circumstances, but I was so intimidated I was not very assertive in my demand.

She asked: "You plead guilty and you don't want to pay the fine?"

I stood there like a moron. I could almost hear people whispering: "Who does he think he is?"

I gave up. Any serious altercation with her highness might result in contempt of court. I pleaded guilty and paid the fines in full.

It seems to me that a magistrate's job requires a limited vocabulary and little decision-making. Besides, the job comes with winning every argument and being fawned over by all those around them.

I want that job. I would even do it for free.

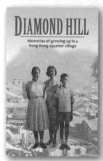